26 JAN 2019
11/2/19.

25 MAY 2019

D0767734

WEST WICKHAM 10/18
020 8777 4139

Please return/renew this item
by the last date shown.
Books may also be renewed by
phone and Internet.

EYEWITNESS TRAVEL

TOP 10
SAN FRANCISCO

JEFFREY KENNEDY

Penguin
Random
House

Top 10 San Francisco Highlights

The Top 10 of Everything

CONTENTS

San Francisco Area by Area

Streetsmart

Within each Top 10 list in this book, no hierarchy of quality or popularity is implied. All 10 are, in the editor's opinion, of roughly equal merit.
   Throughout this book, floors are referred to in accordance with American usage; i.e., the "first floor" is at ground level.

Front cover and spine *A cable car on a street in San Francisco, with the Bay Bridge in the background*
Back cover *Golden Gate Bridge from Marshall Beach*
Title page *Downtown San Francisco skyline with the Transamerica Pyramid*

The information in this DK Eyewitness Top 10 Travel Guide is checked annually. Every effort has been made to ensure that this book is as up-to-date as possible at the time of going to press. Some details, however, such as telephone numbers, opening hours, prices, gallery hanging arrangements, and travel information are liable to change. The publishers cannot accept responsibility for any consequences arising from the use of this book, nor for any material on third-party websites, and cannot guarantee that any website address in this book will be a suitable source of travel information. We value the views and suggestions of our readers very highly. Please write to: Publisher, DK Eyewitness Travel Guides, Dorling Kindersley, 80 Strand, London WC2R 0RL, UK, or email travelguides@dk.com

Welcome to
San Francisco

The glowing Golden Gate Bridge, spanning the stunning Bay, is the quintessential image of San Francisco, but this vibrant city has so much more to offer – from the clacking wheels of cable cars to the smell of steaming crab pots, red and gold pagodas to grand Victorian mansions – and, with Eyewitness Top 10 San Francisco, it's yours to explore.

The misty hills of San Francisco have known Spanish conquistadors, Mexican settlers, the fortune seekers of the Gold Rush, and today's lively Latin American, European, Filipino, Russian, and Pan-Asian populations – each with their own festivals, neighborhoods, and eateries. Cultural diversity in this town is impossible to ignore – just walk down the street to hear a babble of languages. **North Beach** is home to Italians, the **Mission** is Hispanic and Asian, and **Chinatown** speaks for itself. The variety of ethnic restaurants is vast – there are over 4,500 places to eat in this foodie town: sushi bars, *taquerías*, dim sum parlors, brasseries, and Michelin-starred restaurants.

The city shines with culture, from the **San Francisco Museum of Modern Art** and the **de Young Museum** to opera in **Golden Gate Park** and the **Fillmore Jazz Festival**. To intrepid explorers, the city reveals her more hidden treasures, from the backstreet **Tin How Temple** to the cypress-tree sculptures in the **Presidio** forest. The city's annual events are legendary: the **Bay to Breakers** race, the explosive **Chinese New Year** parade, and of course the dazzling pageantry of the **San Francisco Pride parade**.

Whether you're coming for a weekend or a week, our Top 10 guide brings together the best of everything the city has to offer, from iconic sights like **Alcatraz** to day trips to the **Wine Country**. It gives you tips throughout, from things to do for free to how to avoid the crowds, plus easy-to-follow itineraries, planned to help you visit a clutch of sights in a short space of time. Add inspiring photography and detailed maps, and you've got the essential pocket-sized travel companion. **Enjoy the book, and enjoy San Francisco.**

Clockwise from top: **Golden Gate Bridge, statue at the Palace of Fine Arts, a cable car, sailing by Alcatraz, Golden Gate Park, sea lions at Pier 39, detail of City Hall's interior**

Exploring San Francisco

From the back alleys of Chinatown to the Pacific shores, San Francisco offers visitors everything from historic sites and museums to cruises in the vast Bay. Here are some ideas for making the most of your stay, whether you have a weekend to fit in the "must sees," or have enough time for day trips and exploring the city's hidden gems.

Pagoda, Japanese Tea Garden

Ferry Building

Two Days in San Francisco

Day ❶
MORNING

Start the day at **Fisherman's Wharf** *(see pp16–17)* where the Eagle Café on the second floor of **Pier 39** *(see p16)* serves American breakfasts with Bay views. Then take the **Cable Car** to **Union Square** *(see p89)*, where luxury department stores and boutiques glitter around the historic plaza.

AFTERNOON

Walk a few blocks to **Yerba Buena Gardens** *(see pp34–5)*, a sprawling park and arts mecca. Highlights include **SFMOMA** *(see pp32–3)* and a state-of-the-art movie theater at **Metreon** *(see p34)*. Just across

the street is the **Contemporary Jewish Museum (CJM)** *(see p35)*. End the day with dinner in **Chinatown** *(see pp22–3)*.

Day ❷
MORNING

After a Dungeness crab omelette and Irish coffee at **The Buena Vista Café** *(see p101)*, take a ferry across the Bay to **Alcatraz** *(see pp18–19)* for a tour of the historic prison; the audio guide is a must.

AFTERNOON

Walk or bike across the **Golden Gate Bridge** *(see pp12–13)* and back, then stroll on the shoreline past **Crissy Field** *(see p98)*, **Marina Green** *(see p56)*, **Aquatic Park** *(see p98)*, and the **Maritime National Historical Park** *(see p17)*, followed by a seafood feast at **Scoma's** *(see p101)*.

Four Days in San Francisco

Day ❶
MORNING

In **Golden Gate Park** *(see pp24–5)*, take tea in the **Japanese Tea Garden** *(see p24)*. Nearby is the **de Young Museum** *(see pp28–9)*. Enjoy lunch on the terrace of its sculpture garden.

Key
— Two-day itinerary
— Four-day itinerary

AFTERNOON

Explore the rainforest and the living roof at the **California Academy of Sciences** *(see pp26–7)*, row around **Stow Lake** *(see p24)*, and admire the **Dutch Windmill** *(see p24)*. Have dinner at **Cliff House** *(see p123)*.

Day ❷
MORNING

Learn about early California history at the oldest building in the city, **Mission Dolores** *(see p109)*, before heading to a sidewalk table at **Caffè Trieste** *(see p76)* in North Beach for a pizza slice, focaccia sandwich, and a cappuccino. Up the street, the spires of Saints Peter and Paul Church *(see p92)* tower over **Washington Square**, while **Coit Tower** *(see p92)* has Depression-era murals.

AFTERNOON

Head to **Yerba Buena Gardens** *(see pp34–5)* and explore **SFMOMA** *(see pp32–3)* and the other museums, galleries, and gardens. Afterwards, walk to **Chinatown** *(see pp22–3)* and discover the **Tin How Temple** *(see p62)*. Enjoy the multitude of classic Shanghai dumplings on offer at **Yank Sing** *(see p95)*.

Day ❸
MORNING

Take in the woodlands, vistas, and Civil War sites of **The Presidio** *(see p56)*. Savor a Mexican lunch at the impressive **Officers' Club**.

AFTERNOON

Explore **Fisherman's Wharf** *(see pp16–17)*, being sure not to miss the sea lions at **Pier 39** *(see p16)*. Then take a ferry across the Bay to **Alcatraz** *(see pp18–19)* for a tour of the prison. End the day with a ride in a **Cable Car** to **Union Square** *(see p89)* for dinner.

Day ❹
MORNING

Cross the **Golden Gate Bridge** *(see pp12–13)* and drive an hour north to the **Wine Country** *(see pp36–9)*. Visit the **Hess Collection** *(see p37)* to enjoy a winery tour and tasting.

AFTERNOON

Relax in the spas and eateries of **Yountville** *(see p36)* before returning to the city and **Nob Hill** *(see p87)* for cocktails at the **InterContinental Mark Hopkins** *(see p145)*.

Sea lions basking at Pier 39

Top 10 San Francisco Highlights

The living roof of the California Academy of Sciences

TOP 10 San Francisco Highlights

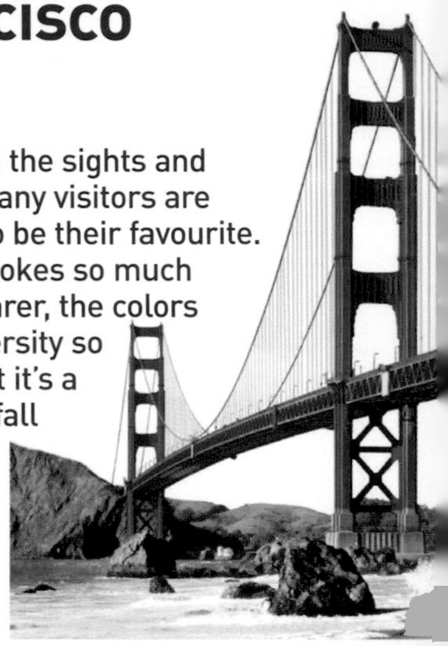

After a few days of taking in the sights and sounds of San Francisco, many visitors are likely to proclaim this city to be their favourite. The geographical setting evokes so much drama, the light seems clearer, the colors more vivid, the cultural diversity so captivating and inviting, that it's a place almost everyone can fall in love with at first sight.

Golden Gate Bridge 1

This symbol of the city is one of the world's largest single span bridges *(see pp12–13)*.

2 Cable Cars

These little troopers now form the world's only system of its kind that still plays a daily role in urban life *(see pp14–15)*.

Van Ness Ave. California
49
& Market Streets

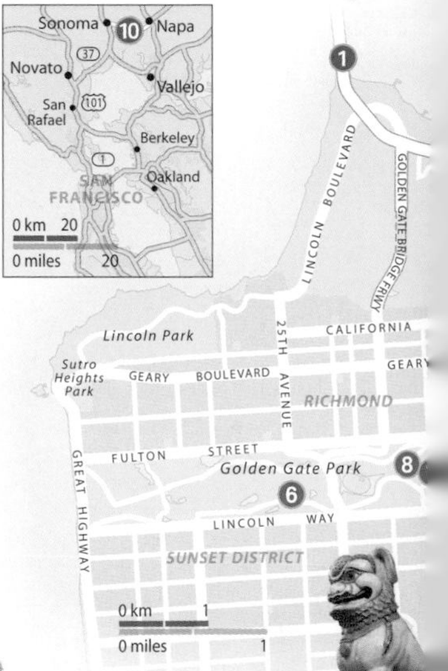
Sonoma
10
Napa
37
Novato
Vallejo
San Rafael
101
Berkeley
1
San Francisco
Oakland
0 km 20
0 miles 20
1
Lincoln Boulevard
Golden Gate Bridge Frwy
California
Lincoln Park
25th Avenue
Sutro Heights Park
Geary Boulevard
Geary
Richmond
Fulton Street
Great Highway
Golden Gate Park
8
6
Lincoln Way
Sunset District
0 km 1
0 miles 1

3 Fisherman's Wharf

The views from here are unmatched. You can also see sea lions and try great seafood *(see pp16–17)*.

Alcatraz 4

"The Rock" continues to capture the imagination. The views from the ferry are worth the visit alone *(see pp18–21)*.

Chinatown 5

The exotic feel of one of the world's largest Chinese communities outside of Asia makes this a magnet for locals and visitors alike *(see pp22–3)*.

Golden Gate Park ⑥

The city boasts one of the world's largest public parks, with natural beauty and fine museums *(see pp24–5)*.

⑧ de Young Museum

A cultural landmark housing American, Oceanian, and African art, as well as temporary exhibits *(see pp28–9)*.

⑦ California Academy of Sciences

This site houses a planetarium, aquarium, and natural history museum under one living roof *(see pp26–7)*.

⑨ SFMOMA

An architectural landmark of the city, SFMOMA houses digital installations and 20th-century masterworks of painting, sculpture and photography, as well as temporary exhibitions *(see pp32–5)*.

⑩ The Wine Country

This picturesque area of Northern California produces some exceptionally fine wines *(see pp36–9)*.

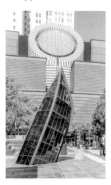

TOP 10 ⭐ Golden Gate Bridge

As with most of the world's wonders, many said the Golden Gate Bridge could never be built – the span was too wide, the ocean too deep, and the cost too great. In 1872, railroad tycoon Charles Crocker conceived the idea, but it took a visionary engineer, Joseph Strauss, to put forth a realistic proposal in 1921. After 10 years of opposition, funding was finally secured. The bridge opened in 1937, and has been an emblem of San Francisco, and America's icon on the Pacific, ever since.

1 Deco Style
The bridge **(right)** owes its striking style to the consulting architect Irving F. Morrow. He simplified the pedestrian railings to uniform posts placed far enough apart to allow for unobstructed, breathtaking views.

2 Bridge Celebrations
The bridge opened on May 27, 1937, with some 200,000 pedestrians. Fifty years later, the ritual was repeated. On May 27, 2012, the 75th anniversary of the opening was marked.

3 Fort Point Lookout
This National Historic Site **(left)** was completed in 1861. It offers soaring views of the underside of the bridge and of the pounding waters of the ocean.

5 Maintenance
Repairing and painting the bridge **(below)** is an ongoing task. The paint protects it from the high salt content in the air, which corrodes the steel components.

4 Toll System
Since 1937, cars have had to pay a toll to cross the bridge. Now, only city-bound traffic is charged, and in 2013 the system was made fully electronic in order to ease the traffic congestion from stopping at toll booths.

8 Building the Bridge

Strauss introduced the use of hard hats **(above)** and a safety net that saved 19 workers' lives.

9 Hiking and Biking

Every visitor should walk or cycle across at least part of the bridge.

10 Marin Vista Point

Crossing over to the north side, pull off just before the end to take in the startling panorama from the Vista Point. Look back at the hills and spires of the city.

6 Star Turns in Movies

The bridge has starred in many movies, most notably Alfred Hitchcock's *Vertigo*, in which James Stewart pulls Kim Novak from the raging surf, just east of Fort Point *(see p98)*. In *A View to a Kill* **(right)**, 007 and Christopher Walken battle it out, both clinging to its aerial heights.

7 Protective Barriers

The Golden Gate Bridge is the number-two spot in the world for suicides. As yet there have been no barriers effective enough to prevent this, but there are bars in place for general safety.

THE STATISTICS

The length of the steel wires used to make the cables of the bridge is enough to circle the earth three times. It is also brilliantly "over-engineered" and is said to be five times stronger than it needs to be to withstand the winds and tides it endures daily. At the time it was built, it was the longest suspension bridge in the world (it now ranks twelfth) and took just over four years to build. About 40 million vehicles cross the bridge annually, streaming across six lanes of traffic, along its 1.7-mile (2.7-km) length. The bridge is equipped with two foghorns, each with a different pitch, and 360-degree flashing red beacons. The bridge has been closed due to high winds only three times in its history.

NEED TO KNOW

Map C1

■ (415) 921-5858

■ www.goldengate.org

■ For a uniquely powerful view of the bridge, while enjoying a Sunday champagne brunch, opt for one of the many cruises around the Bay, departing from the Embarcadero Pier and Sausalito. Quality purveyors are Hornblower Cruises ((415) 788-8866, www.hornblower.com), and Call of the Sea/Seaward ((415) 331-3214, www.callofthesea.org).

🔟⭐ Cable Cars

It's impossible not to love these vestiges of another age, as they valiantly make their way up the precipitous hills. Yet they came perilously close to being scrapped in 1947, when a "progressive" mayor announced it was time for buses to take their place. An outraged citizenry prevailed, and the system was declared a National Historic Landmark in 1964. In the early 1980s, it underwent a $60 million overhaul. The present service of about 40 cars covers some 10 miles (16 km).

1 Bell
While operating up and down the hills, the cable car's bell **(right)** is used by the grip person like a klaxon, to warn other vehicles and pedestrians of imminent stops, starts, and turns.

2 Grip Person
The grip person **(below)** must be quick-thinking and strong to operate the heavy gripping levers and braking mechanisms. The grip is like a huge pair of pliers that clamps onto the cable to pull the car along.

3 Cars
Cable cars **(right)** come in two types: one that has a turnaround system, one that does not. All of them are numbered, have wood-and-brass fittings in the 19th-century style, and are often painted in differing colors.

4 Conductor
Collects fares, but also makes sure that everyone travels safely, and that the grip person has room to work.

5 Braking
Wheel brakes press against the wheels; track brakes press against the tracks when the grip person pulls a lever; the emergency brake is a steel wedge forced into the rail slot.

6 Riding Styles
There is a choice of sitting inside a glassed-in compartment, sitting outside on wooden benches, or hanging onto poles and standing on the running board. The third option is the best one for enjoying the enticing sights, sounds, and smells of San Francisco.

CABLE CARS AND STREETCARS

Andrew Hallidie's cable car system dates from August 2, 1873, when he tested his prototype based on mining cars. It was an immediate success and spawned imitators in more than a dozen cities worldwide. However, 20 years later, it was set to be replaced by the electric streetcar. Fortunately, resistance to above-ground wires, corruption in City Hall, and finally the 1906 earthquake, sidetracked those plans. The cable car was kept for the steepest lines, while the streetcar took over the longer, flatter routes.

8 Turntables
Part of the fun of the cable car experience is being there to watch when the grip person and conductor turn their car around for the return trip **(left)**. The best view is at Powell and Market Streets.

9 Cable Car Museum
Downstairs, look at the giant sheaves (wheels), which keep the cables moving throughout the system **(above)**; upstairs there are displays of some of the earliest cable cars.

10 Routes
The three existing routes cover the Financial District, Nob Hill **(below)**, Chinatown, North Beach, Russian Hill, and Fisherman's Wharf areas. As these are always important destinations for visitors – and for many residents, too – most people will find that a cable car ride is a practical, as well as a pleasurable, experience.

7 Cables
The underground cables are 1.25 inches (3 cm) in diameter and consist of six steel strands of 19 wires, wrapped around a shock-absorbing rope.

NEED TO KNOW

MAP M3

Cable Car Museum: 1201 Mason St at Washington; (415) 474-1887; open Apr–Sep: 10am–6pm daily; Oct–Mar: 10am–5pm daily; www. cablecarmuseum.org

■ Rather than wait in the long lines at a cable car terminus, do what the locals do and walk up a stop or two, where you can hop on right away for a $7 fee – then hold on!

■ The $7 fare is for one ride, in one direction, with no transfers. Consider getting a CityPass or a Muni Passport for one day ($20) or longer *(see pp134–5)*.

Fisherman's Wharf

Tourists, enjoying takeout crab cocktails and sourdough bread, crowd the sidewalks and souvenir stands of the old seaside wharf district. Amid today's seafood eateries, aquarium, wax museum, and Bay cruise piers, fishing boats become great photo ops as their catches of Dungeness crab and Pacific fish are unloaded. The rowdy old days of the 1850s are reenacted on masted schooners, while a World War II-era submarine and a Liberty ship recall the city's long history as a major port.

PIER 39 ①
One of the most popular attractions in the city is set on a land-scaped pier with dazzling Bay views, restaurants, live entertainment, and shops **(right)**. Get discount coupons at the California Welcome Center. Families love the bungee jump, mirror maze, games arcade, and carousel.

② **Ghirardelli Square**
The Ghirardelli family used this square as the headquarters of the Ghirardelli Chocolate Company from 1859 until 1962. The site is now home to upscale shops and eateries *(see p100)*.

③ **Aquarium of the Bay**
The transparent tunnel of the aquarium visually immerses you in the San Francisco Bay marine habitat, where thousands of different species of spectacular ocean fauna disport themselves before your eyes. Video presentations and marine specialist guides help you to understand what you're seeing.

Anchorage Square Shopping Center ④
In the heart of Fisherman's Wharf, with plenty of stores, restaurants, and entertainment **(right)**.

⑤ **Boudin Bakery**
This is the home of the famous chain of San Francisco sourdough breadmakers **(left)**. Try the crusty round loaf, best enjoyed warm from the oven with plenty of butter.

⑥ **Madame Tussauds**
Incredibly lifelike wax figures of movie stars, music legends, political and sports icons, and San Francisco celebrities are on display here. A scary "Dungeon" theatrical show is for ages 10 and up.

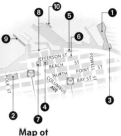

**Map of
Fisherman's Wharf**

7 The Cannery

Built as a warehouse in 1907, the building underwent a makeover in 1967, and it's now the site of some appealing boutiques, as well as tourist shops.

8 Fish Alley

This alley is possibly the last vestige of the authentic, workaday wharf. Here you can see fishing boats come in and watch as the catch of the day is landed and prepared for market.

9 Maritime National Historical Park

At the Hyde Street Pier **(below)** are vessels ranging from 1880s schooners and a spectacular 1886 square-rigger to 1900s tugs and the USS *Pampanito* World War II submarine.

THE PORT OF SAN FRANCISCO

Born of the California Gold Rush of 1849, the Port of San Francisco **(below)** stretches nearly 8 miles (13 km) from the Hyde Street Pier to India Basin. A cruise ship terminal hosts 80 cruise ship calls and 300,000 passengers annually, while freighters lumber under the Golden Gate Bridge and ferries, water taxis, fishing boats, and yachts bustle to and from the Ferry Building, Fisherman's Wharf, and Embarcadero piers and marinas.

10 SS Jeremiah O'Brien Liberty Ship

At Pier 45 floats this fully restored World War II Liberty ship. Take a free tour to hear tales of the thousands of troops ferried across the seas.

NEED TO KNOW

MAP J3

Aquarium of the Bay: Embarcadero; (415) 623-5300; open 9am–8pm daily (winter: 10am–6pm Mon–Thu, 10am–7pm Fri–Sun); adm $14.95–$25.95; www.aquariumofthebay.org

Anchorage Sq Shopping Center: 333 Jefferson St; (415) 775-6000; www.anchoragesquare.com

Madame Tussauds: 145 Jefferson St; (866)223-4240; open 10am–9pm Sun–Thu, 10am–10pm Fri–Sat; adm $15.99–$19.99; www.madametussauds.com

Maritime National Historical Park: 499 Jefferson St; open 9:30am–5pm daily; adm $10; under-16s free; www.maritime.org

SS Jeremiah O'Brien Liberty Ship: Pier 45; (415) 544-0100; open 9am–4pm daily; adm $10–$20; under-5s free; www.ssjeremiahobrien.org

■ For some of the best seafood in the city, head straight to Scoma's – the culinary stalwart (see p101).

🔟⭐ Alcatraz

To the inmates physically confined on this island prison, their punishment was also psychological. They were in the midst of one of America's busiest harbors, and could probably hear the ceaseless procession of cars crossing the bridges and honking their horns. They could certainly see the ocean liners gliding to faraway ports. These were all reminders that life was near, but freedom very far.

THE HISTORY OF "THE ROCK"

The name "Alcatraz" derives from the Spanish *alcatraces*, for the birds that Spanish explorer Juan Manuel de Ayala observed here when he sailed into the Bay in 1775. In 1850, the island was set aside for the US Army to build a citadel, but defense became less of a priority and, in 1907, it became a military prison. In 1934 the Federal Government opened a maximum-security penitentiary here. Yet Alcatraz was not the "Devil's Island" that many think it was – the conditions were better than many other prisons.

1 Chapel
Above the guardhouse, a Mission-style military chapel **(above)** was built in the 1920s. It was also used as living quarters and a school. During the post-1930s prison phase, it housed prison staff.

2 Tours
Rangers lead free guided tours focusing on the Native American Occupation, the gardens, birdwatching, and more.

3 Recreation Yard
Good behavior qualified prisoners for a turn around the walled-in recreation yard **(left)**. Here, they could walk outside of their cells, where they spent between 16 and 23 hours a day.

4 Lighthouse
Alcatraz was the site of the first lighthouse built on the West Coast in 1854. The original was replaced in 1909 to tower above the new cell block **(above)**.

5 Control Room
Guards controlled the security system from this bunker-like facility **(above)**. Next to the Control Room was the visiting area, where thick glass separated prisoners and visitors, and conversations were held over telephones.

6 Broadway
The corridor that separates C and B blocks was jokingly nick-named by prisoners after New York City's glittering thoroughfare, famous for its nightlife. The intersection at the end was named "Times Square."

7 Cell Blocks
The cell house contains four free-standing cell blocks **(below)**. The complex was built by military prisoners in 1911 and was once the largest reinforced concrete building in the world. In all, there were 390 cells, but the prison population averaged only about 260 at any one time.

NEED TO KNOW

Alcatraz Cruises (Hornblower) from Pier 33: (415) 981-7625 (tickets and schedules) ▪ www.alcatrazcruises.com

Open daily

Adm: day tours: $37.25 adult, $35.25 senior, $23 child 5–11 years; night tours: $44.25 adult, $41.25 senior, $26.50 child 5–11 years; family packages available

Tour compulsory

▪ Picnicking is allowed on the dock, but you'll have to bring your own food.

▪ The weather is often blustery and cold on the island, and the trails and walkways rough. Wear warm clothes and strong, comfortable shoes.

▪ A cell-house audio tour explores the prison and its stories. It is available in eleven languages and is included in the price of the ticket, as is the excellent ranger-guided tour.

9 Mess Hall
Meals were one of the few things prisoners had to look forward to, and they were generally well fed to quell rebellion. Note the sample menu at the entrance to the kitchen **(below)**.

8 Warden's House
Until the house burned down in 1970, the warden's home **(below)** looked out to freedom. Designed in Mission Revival style, the home had 17 large rooms, and sweeping views of the Golden Gate Bridge and San Francisco's lights.

10 Building 64
The theater and orientation center are located in the old bar-racks building behind the ferry jetty. The building also houses a bookstore, exhibits, and a multimedia show providing a historical overview of Alcatraz.

Stories from The Rock

Burt Lancaster in *Birdman of Alcatraz*

1 Robert "Birdman" Stroud

The most famous inmate was dubbed the "Birdman of Alcatraz," despite the fact that he was not permitted to conduct his avian studies during his 17 years here. Due to his violent nature, Stroud spent most of those years in solitary.

2 Birdman of Alcatraz

This 1962 movie presented Robert Stroud as a nature-loving ornithologist, bending historical fact to the service of a good story.

3 Al Capone

In 1934 Capone was among the first "official" shipment of prisoners. The infamous gangster was assigned menial jobs and treated like every other inmate.

4 George "Machine Gun" Kelly

Jailed in 1933 for kidnapping, Kelly was given a life sentence, and was sent to Alcatraz for 17 years of his sentence. He was considered a model prisoner by the officers.

5 Alvin "Creepy" Karpis

Karpis robbed his way through the Midwest between 1931 and 1936, and earned himself the title Public Enemy Number One. He was imprisoned on Alcatraz from 1936 to 1962. He committed suicide in 1979.

6 Morton Sobell

Charged with conspiracy to commit treason by spying for the Soviets, Sobell arrived on Alcatraz in 1952 and spent five years as its most famous political prisoner, being a victim of J. Edgar Hoover's witch hunt for Communist subversives. Once freed, Sobell returned to live in San Francisco for many years.

7 Anglin Brothers

The brothers, John and Clarence, are notable as two of the five known inmates to successfully escape from The Rock.

Clint Eastwood in *Escape from Alcatraz*

8 Escape from Alcatraz

Starring Clint Eastwood as Frank Morris, who escaped along with the Anglin brothers. Again, this 1979 film is largely Hollywood fiction. However, the depiction of prison life is reportedly accurate.

9 Frank Watherman

The last prisoner to leave Alcatraz, on March 21, 1963.

10 The Rock

Hollywood has never lost its fascination with Alcatraz, as can be seen in this 1996 action thriller, starring Sean Connery.

NATIVE AMERICAN OCCUPATION

In 1969 Richard Oakes and 90 other Native Americans landed on Alcatraz, set up camp, and demanded that the government sell them the island for $24 worth of beads and red cloth. They claimed that this was the price their people had been paid in exchange for an island similar in size nearly 300 years earlier. The government considered forcibly removing the occupiers, but growing public support for the Native Americans forced officials to renew negotiations. However, in January, 1970, while playing on the rooftop of one of the buildings, Oakes' youngest daughter slipped and fell to her death; distraught, he and his family decided to abandon their claim. Sixty Native Americans remained, but as the stalemate dragged on, the majority slowly began to leave – only 15 chose to stay. In June, 1970, fires ravaged the warden's house, the recreation hall, the officers' club, and the lighthouse. Following this devastation, government troops staged a pre-dawn raid. The remaining Native Americans were arrested and the 19-month occupation came to an end.

John Anglin, escaped June, 1962

TOP 10 ESCAPE ATTEMPTS

1 December, 1937: Theodore Cole and Ralph Roe

2 May, 1938: Thomas Limerick, James Lucas, and Rufus Franklin

3 January, 1939: Arthur "Doc" Barker, Dale Stamphill, William Martin, Henry Young, and Rufus McCain

4 May, 1941: Joseph Cretzer, Sam Shockley, Arnold Kyle, and Lloyd Barkdoll

5 April, 1943: James Boarman, Harold Brest, Floyd Hamilton, and Fred Hunter

6 July, 1945: John Giles

7 May, 1946: Bernard Coy, Joseph Cretzer, Marvin Hubbard, Sam Shockley, Miran Thompson, and Clarence Carnes

8 September, 1958: Aaron Burgett and Clyde Johnson

9 June, 1962: Frank Morris and John and Clarence Anglin

10 December, 1962: John Paul Scott and Darl Parker

Native American in full ceremonial attire as he stands in an open cell in the former Alcatraz Prison during the Native American occupation.

TOP 10 ⭐ **Chinatown**

This teeming, densely populated neighborhood, with its bright facades, noisy markets, exotic temples, and ethnic restaurants and shops, is like a city within the city – and a place every visit to San Francisco must include. The atmosphere recalls a typical southern Chinese town, although the architecture, customs, and public celebrations are distinctly American hybrids on a Cantonese theme. Overlook the tourist tackiness, check out some of the side alleys, and give yourself time to take it all in.

Chinatown Gate ①
A gift from Taiwan in 1970, this triple-pagoda southern entrance to Chinatown **(right)** was inspired by traditional Chinese village gates.

② **Golden Gate Fortune Cookie Company**
Fortune cookies were invented in San Francisco. Stop by to watch how the skilful workers slip the fortune message in the cookie mixture then fold it into the traditional shapes.

③ **Chinese Six Companies**
This building's brilliant facade is one of the most ornate in Chinatown. The Six Companies association was formed in 1882 to promote Chinese interests within the community.

④ **Portsmouth Square**
This was San Francisco's original town square – here, on July 9, 1846, the US flag was first raised when the port was seized from Mexico. Locals now use the area for tai chi and games of mah-jongg **(below)**.

⑤ **St. Mary's Square**
This square is graced by a stainless-steel and rose-granite statue of Sun Yat-sen by San Francisco sculptor Beniamino Bufano.

⑥ **Chinese Historical Society of America**
This building, designed by architect Julia Morgan in 1932, is the home of a learning center and a museum containing a 15,000-piece collection of artifacts, documents, photographs, and replicas that illustrate and explain the Chinese-American experience.

7 Stockton Street Chinese Markets

At these authentic markets **(left)** selling fresh produce, the real smells, sights, and sounds of Chinatown come into sharp focus.

8 Old Chinese Telephone Exchange

This three-tiered pagoda is now the East West Bank, and is the most distinctive work of architectural chinoiserie in Chinatown. It served as the telephone exchange up until the 1950s.

9 Chinese Culture Center

The Chinese Culture Center comprises an art gallery and a small crafts shop, which features the work of Chinese and Chinese-American artists.

10 Temples

There are a number of temples that incorporate Confucian, Taoist, and Buddhist elements. The Tin How Temple **(right)**, founded in 1852, is particularly worth visiting (see p62).

GOLD RUSH CANTONESE

Chinese immigrants began to arrive with the Gold Rush, to get rich quick and return home heroes. As it happened, things turned politically sour in China at the time, and many Chinese people stayed in the new land. There was, however, a racist backlash against them, resulting in the Chinese Exclusion Act of 1882, and Chinatown became a kind of ghetto, full of opium dens and vice. The act was repealed in 1943, and things have steadily improved ever since.

NEED TO KNOW

MAP N4

Golden Gate Fortune Cookie Company: **MAP M4** ▪ 56 Ross Alley ▪ (415) 781-3956

Chinese Six Companies: **MAP N4** ▪ 843 Stockton St

Chinese Historical Society of America: **MAP N5** ▪ 965 Clay St ▪ (415) 391-1188 ▪ www.chsa.org

Old Chinese Telephone Exchange: **MAP M4** ▪ 743 Washington St

Chinese Culture Center: **MAP M5** ▪ Hilton Hotel, 750 Kearny St, 3rd floor ▪ (415) 986-1822 ▪ www.c-c-c.org

▪ Don't drive into Chinatown: it's very congested, and it can be impossible to find parking. Take the cable car instead. All three of the cable car lines will get you to the area (see p15).

▪ One of the most popular Chinese restaurants in San Francisco, Yank Sing, can be found here (see p95). It serves authentic Shanghai dumplings. There are also plenty of other classic Asian eateries to choose from.

TOP 10 ⭐ Golden Gate Park

This is every San Franciscan's beloved backyard. Weekends draw hundreds of people here to play or relax. Almost every sort of recreational activity is available, from hiking to fishing. There's also the very first children's playground in the US, with the magnificent Herschell-Spillman Carousel, built in 1914 *(see p67)*. Even on a rainy day, the park offers world-class activities in the form of de Young Museum *(see pp28–9)*, the California Academy of Sciences *(see pp26–7)*, and Morrison Planetarium.

1 National AIDS Memorial Grove

This memorial, in a quiet forest hideaway, was built in remembrance of those who have died from AIDS.

2 Stow Lake and Strawberry Hill

Strawberry Hill is the island in the middle of this lake. Don't miss the Chinese moon-viewing pavilion on the island's eastern shore.

3 Conservatory of Flowers

The park's oldest building, a copy of one in London's Kew Gardens, is a Victorian Structure sheltering over 20,000 rare and exotic plants.

4 Japanese Tea Garden

This delightful garden is full of bonsai trees, rock gardens, exotic plantings, and pagodas **(right)**.

5 Bison Paddock

In 1984 a small herd of bison was given a home roaming under the eucalyptus trees.

6 Strybing Arboretum and Botanical Garden

More than 7,000 species live in areas including a Redwood Grove, an Ancient Plant Garden, and a Garden of Fragrance.

7 Giant Tree Fern Grove and John McLaren Rhododendron Dell

Coming upon the Giant Tree Fern Grove, with its huge, curling proto-flora gathered around a small lagoon, is like entering a primeval forest. The Rhododendron Dell contains the largest variety (850) of these blooms in any US garden.

8 Dutch Windmill and Queen Wilhelmina Tulip Garden

In the northwest corner of the park, the gigantic windmill towers over the stunning tulip garden that surrounds it **(left)**. Both were gifts from the queen of the Netherlands in 1902.

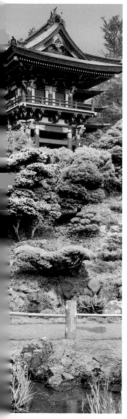

⑩ Shakespeare Garden

This charming English garden **(above)** features the 200-odd flowers and herbs mentioned in the Bard's works. Bronze plaques quote the relevant passages.

Music Concourse ⑨

This area **(right)** hosts free events and summer concerts by the San Francisco Opera.

A MIRACLE OF LAND RECLAMATION

The park's more than 1.5 sq miles (4 sq km) are some 3 miles (5 km) long and half a mile (1 km) wide, making it the largest cultivated urban park in the US. There are 27 miles (43 km) of footpaths, winding through lakes, gardens, waterfalls, and forests, but it was not always so. Before the 1870s, the entire area was sandy wastes and scrubland. William Hammond Hall made great progress over two decades, then hired Scottish gardener John McLaren in 1890. "Uncle John," as he was known, made the park his life's work, devoting himself to its perfection until his death in 1943, aged 97.

TOP 10 ⭐ California Academy of Sciences

Located in Golden Gate Park since 1916, the California Academy of Sciences now occupies a modern building. It houses the Steinhart Aquarium, Morrison Planetarium, and the Kimball Natural History Museum, and combines innovative architecture with flexible exhibition spaces. Filled with native plant species, the 2.5-acre (1-ha) living roof has been designed to help the museum blend in with the surrounding parkland.

1 Living Roof

The museum is topped with a 108,900-sq-ft (10,100-sq-m) living roof (above), which is planted with over 1.7 million native Californian plants. Take an elevator up to the rooftop deck to enjoy the views and learn about the benefits of sustainable architecture.

2 California Coast

Explore habitats ranging from salt marshes to turbulent rocky inlets and meet a variety of native fish and invertebrates. The main tank – an exhibit featuring the marine habitats of the Gulf of the Farallones National Marine Sanctuary – is 100,000 gallons in capacity, with large viewing windows, and a crashing wave surge system.

3 Discovery Tidepool

Stroke a starfish or pick up a sea slug in this hands-on attraction, which is part of the California Coast exhibits. You don't have to worry about slippery rocks to get close to these coastal creatures. The pool is staffed by volunteers who inform you about the animals and keep them safe.

4 Morrison Planetarium

Fly through space and time to the very limits of the known universe, and gain a new perspective on the planet we call home, with high-tech exhibits and technology, including an all-digital dome (below). Shows are presented daily.

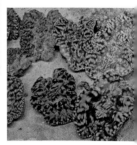

8 The Swamp
Part of the Steinhart Aquarium, which holds about 38,000 animals from around the world, the Swamp is home to alligator snapping turtles, Claude (the famous albino alligator), and exhibits of frogs, rattlesnakes, and salamanders.

9 Philippine Coral Reef
This is one of the deepest living coral reef displays in the world. It exhibits a range of aquatic life from the reefs and mangroves of the Philippines. Sharks, rays, coral, reef fish, and colorful clams **(below)** can all be seen here.

5 Osher Rainforest
Explore four rainforest habitats in a large glass dome: the Amazonian Flooded Forest, Borneo Forest Floor, Madagascar Rainforest Understory, and the Costa Rica Rainforest Canopy. The path **(above)** winds up in a habitat of 1,600 tropical plants and creatures, such as piranhas, flying lizards, birds, and an Amazonian boa.

7 African Hall
Magnificent dioramas display a range of African fauna in their natural surroundings, such as the straight-horned oryx, gorillas, antelope **(below)**, and cheetahs. The human evolution exhibit tracks the fascinating history of our species with fossils of our early ancestors. A colony of African penguins, which is viewed through a vast window, ends the exhibit.

10 Water Planet
Dozens of tanks and a range of interactive media are used to inform all ages of what it takes to survive under water. A variety of fish, including jellyfish, paddlefish, reptiles like zebra morays, amphibians, and insects are on display.

6 Penguin Feeding Time
Enjoy watching the black-footed penguins waddle on land, or dive and glide effortlessly through the water to catch their meal, in the African Hall.

🔟⭐ de Young Museum

The immense copper-clad de Young Museum looms as a cultural and architectural landmark above a canopy of plane trees in the Music Concourse of the Golden Gate Park. It is a bastion of American, Oceanian, and African art, as well as housing a world-famous textile collection. The de Young also lures crowds to blockbuster temporary exhibits such as the Oscar de la Renta retrospective, the multimedia Summer of Love Experience, and archeological finds from the ancient Mexican city of Teotihuacan.

1 Textiles and Costumes

Three centuries of fiber art and fashion include bark cloth, Central Asian and North Indian silks, the most important Anatolian kilims outside Turkey (above), European tapestries, and early 20th-century couture.

2 Hamon Observation Tower

It's free to ascend the 144-ft (43.8-m) tower to the 360-degree glass-walled observation deck (below) for treetop views of the Music Concourse, the park, the city, and beyond to the Golden Gate Bridge and the Marin Headlands.

3 Photography

Spanning the history of the medium, the de Young is strong on 19th-century American and European images, from documentation of the 1894 California Midwinter International Exposition and daguerre-otypes to early and contemporary San Franciscan scenes.

4 Temporary Exhibits

Wildly popular and requiring advance tickets, some block-buster exhibitions have included Tutankhamun's treasures and retrospectives on artists Ed Ruscha and Frank Stella.

5 20th-Century American and Bay Area Artists

Georgia O'Keeffe's *Petunias* is among the contemporary masterworks on dis-play, along with those of local icons – Chiura Obata, Wayne Thiebaud, and Ruth Asawa. It also features a major acquisition of works by African Americans.

6 Museum Gardens

Explore the remnants of the California Mid-winter International Exposition of 1894 in the surrounding shady walking trails (above): the Pool of Enchantment, the vases, and the sphinxes (left).

7 Artful Kids

The de Young welcomes kids to free Saturday art classes, summer camps, and a monthly artist-in-resi-dence workshop for the whole family. Guided tours for families are followed by studio workshops taught by professional artists.

⑩ American Collection

Founded by donations from the Rockefellers, this comprehensive collection, from 1670 to the present, has more than 3,000 decorative arts objects, 800 sculptures, and 1,000 paintings, including *Boatmen on the Missouri* by George Caleb Bingham **(left)**.

A DAY AT THE DE YOUNG

Take breaks from total art immersion by enjoying the indoor-outdoor café and the rambling sculpture garden (you can come in and out of the museum all day with your ticket). Audio and docent-led tours enrich the experience, as do curator talks and workshops. Art enthusiasts flock to the "Friday Nights at the de Young" events of music, panels, and interaction with artists, during which cocktails are served. The two-level store is stocked with art books, exhibit programs, logo items, and signature jewelry, textiles, posters, and prints relating to the exhibits. Kids can hang out in the toy- and book-filled children's section.

⑧ Art of the Americas

Pre-Columbian and ancient Native American artifacts are displayed in these galleries, including a stunning group of Teotihuacan murals. The Weisel Family Collection spans 1,000 years of Native American objects and textiles.

⑨ Africa and the Pacific

Micronesian and Maori carvings, basketry, and over 1,400 pieces from across the regions are on view **(below)**, along with Scheller's collection of Masterworks of African Figurative Sculpture, depicting 140 ethnic groups.

NEED TO KNOW

MAP C4 ■ 50 Hagiwara Tea Garden Drive, Golden Gate Park ■ (415) 750-3600 ■ www.deyoung.famsf.org

Open 9:30am–5:15pm Tue–Sun; 9:30am–8:30pm on selected Fri (see website for details)

Adm $15 adult, $10 senior, $6 student/youth, free child 0–12 years; free first Tue of month; limited-run exhibitions may require separate tickets purchased in advance.

■ The de Young is accessible via Muni lines 5, 44, and the N-Judah. Save $2 on admission with proof of public transit. Self-parking is available under the museum.

■ Children are welcome, although large bags are forbidden and strollers are not allowed in some venues.

■ Same-day free admission to the Legion of Honor museum (see p117) with a de Young ticket.

Following pages Rolling vineyards in Sonoma County

TOP 10 ★ San Francisco Museum of Modern Art

SFMOMA forms the nucleus of San Francisco's reputation as a leading center of modern art. Created in 1935, it moved into its current quarters in 1995, and in May 2016 reopened after a major three-year $305 million expansion that tripled its gallery space. The museum offers a dynamic schedule of special exhibitions and permanent collection presentations in its 170,000 sq ft (15,795 sq m) gallery space.

1 Outdoor Terraces
Six outdoor terraces provide spaces for sculpture installations and highlight dramatic cityscape views.

2 Photography
A highlight of the museum; the 15,000 sq ft (1, 394 sq m) Pritzker Center for Photography houses a collection of over 17,800 photographs.

3 Exterior
The façade of the Snøhetta expansion (below) comprises more than 700 uniquely-shaped panels which appear to shift in appearance with the changing light.

4 Latin American Artists
Latin American art is represented most forcefully in the museum by the work of muralist Diego Rivera and Frida Kahlo. Other Latin American painters represented include Wifredo Lam and Joaquín Torres-García.

5 Media Arts
Established in 1988, the impressive collection includes multimedia works, moving-image pieces, and video installations by such artists as Brian Eno, Dara Birnbaum, Bill Viola, and Nam June Paik.

6 The Living Wall
This incredible living wall provides a unique background for sculpture on the third floor terrace. Populated with 19,000 plants, including 21 native plant species, it is an ever-changing work of natural art.

7 Special Exhibitions
The museum's special exhibition spaces may feature retrospective exhibitions of the work of modern and contemporary artists, such as multimedia artist Yoko Ono, sculptor Eva Hesse, and artist Robert Rauschenberg.

Key
- First floor
- Second floor
- Third floor
- Fourth floor
- Fifth floor
- Sixth floor
- Seventh floor

SFMOMA Floorplan

Special Exhibitions **7**

Media Arts **5**

Special Exhibitions **7**

Bay Area Artists **10**

Latin American Artists **4**

1 Outdoor Terraces

6 The Living Wall

2 Photography

8 20th-Century European Artists

9 20th-Century American Artists

xterior **3**

NEED TO KNOW

MAP Q5 ■ 151 3rd St ■ (415) 357-4000 ■ www.sfmoma.org

Open 10am–5pm Fri–Tue (until 9pm Thu)

Adm $25 adult, $22 senior (65 years and older), $19 19–24 years with ID, free 18 and under; audio tour price varies

Museum store: open 10am–6pm Fri–Tue, 10am–5pm Wed, 10am–9:30pm Thu

■ Across 3rd Street from SFMOMA, Yerba Buena Gardens *(see pp34–5)* offers more galleries, museums, and attractions.

■ Sightglass at SFMOMA, on the third floor, serves coffee and pastries, whilst family-friendly Cafe 5 is in the sculpture garden. For fine dining, head to In Situ, on the first floor.

Museum Guide

The ground floor welcomes visitors with free art-filled public spaces and galleries. Works from the permanent collection are on the second floor, as are galleries for works on paper and Californian art. The Pritzker Center for Photography is located on the third floor, whilst the Doris and Donald Fisher Collection begins on the third floor and continues in the Fisher Galleries on the fourth, fifth, and sixth floors. The seventh floor showcases contemporary works and media arts.

8 20th-Century European Artists

These works are located on the second floor. Here you will find important works by Matisse, Miró, Klee, Picasso, Braque, Mondrian, Duchamp, Dalí, and Magritte, among others.

9 20th-Century American Artists

US artists included here are O'Keeffe, de Kooning, Pollock, Warhol, and Kline. One of the perennial hits is Jeff Koons' iconic ceramic sculpture *Michael Jackson and Bubbles* (1988) **(right)**.

10 Bay Area Artists

San Francisco Bay Area artists with international reputations on display include Clyfford Still, Richard Diebenkorn, and Wayne Thiebaud. Bay Area figurative painters in the collection include Elmer Bischoff and David Park. Most noteworthy, perhaps, is *California Artist* (1982), a sculptural self-portrait by Robert Arneson in glazed stoneware.

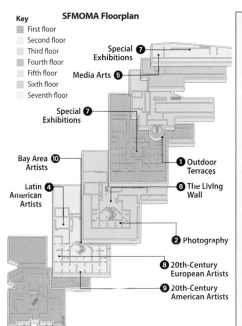

Yerba Buena Gardens

Skyscrapers around Yerba Buena Gardens

① Yerba Buena Center for the Arts Gallery

MAP Q5 ▪ 701 Mission St ▪ (415) 978-2787 ▪ Open noon–6pm Wed & Sun, noon–8pm Thu–Sat ▪ Adm ▪ www.ybca.org

Changing exhibitions here explore issues of race, class, gender, history, technology, and art.

② Yerba Buena Center for the Arts Theater

MAP Q5 ▪ Box Office: (415) 978-2787

Multiculturalism is often the keynote in this 750-seat indoor theater, so that the range of performances could include world-music festivals or Victorian operettas.

③ Moscone Center

MAP Q5 ▪ Howard St

This building began the renovation of the SoMa district. Most of it is under-ground; above ground the impression is of glass, girders, and gardens.

④ Metreon

MAP Q4 ▪ 101 4th St

The main attraction at this shopping center is a state-of-the-art movie theater (including IMAX screens). On the fourth floor is a pleasant terrace with superb views of the cityscape.

⑤ Rooftop Children's Center and Carousel

MAP Q5 ▪ 750 Folsom St

The carousel in this complex dates from 1906. There's also an ice-skating rink, a bowling alley, a learning gar-den, and an amphitheater.

⑥ Children's Creativity Museum

MAP Q5 ▪ 221 4th St ▪ (415) 820-3320 ▪ Open 10am–4pm Wed–Sun ▪ Adm ▪ www.creativity.org

This interactive technology and art museum aims to inspire children's creative impulses. There are anim-ation, design, and music studios.

⑦ California Historical Society

MAP P5 ▪ 678 Mission St ▪ (415) 357-1848 ▪ Open 11am–5pm Tue–Sun ▪ Adm

This research organization holds vast collections of photos, books, maps, manuscripts, prints, and arts, some dating as far back as the 1600s.

⑧ Martin Luther King, Jr. Memorial

Featuring words of peace in several languages, this multifaceted monument incorporates sculpture, a waterfall, and quotations from the speeches and writings of the Civil Rights leader.

⑨ Contemporary Jewish Museum (CJM)

MAP P5 ▪ 736 Mission St between 3rd and 4th ▪ (415) 655-7800 ▪ Open 11am–8pm Thu, 11am–5pm Fri–Tue ▪ Closed Wed, Jewish hols & some public hols ▪ Adm ▪ www.thecjm.org

This dynamic museum was designed by architect Daniel Libeskind and incorporates the landmark Jesse Street Power Substation. Its exhibitions help to make the Jewish experience relatable for the wider 21st-century community *(see p53)*.

Contemporary Jewish Museum

⑩ Esplanade

www.ybgfestival.org

The Esplanade comprises garden-lined walkways, an inviting lawn, rolling hills, trees, and interesting sculptures. There is a free weekly concert here during the summer festival.

THE RISE OF SOUTH OF MARKET

Formerly an unattractive and dangerous industrial area of warehouses and factories, the SoMa district began its transformation in the 1970s, when the slums were cleared away and the Moscone Center was built. Upscale interior designer showrooms emerged, along with trendy nightclubs and restaurants, high-rise hotels and office buildings, as well as museums and galleries. The three buildings of the Moscone Center comprise more than 1,000,000-sq-ft (93,000-sq-m) of exhibition and meeting spaces. The whole district is now seen as a desirable neighborhood – at least for creative types.

TOP 10 NOTABLE CONSTRUCTIONS SOUTH OF MARKET

1 AT&T Park
2 SFMOMA
3 Moscone Center
4 Yerba Buena Center
5 Rincon Center
6 Metreon
7 South Park
8 The Galleria
9 Millennium Tower
10 The Four Seasons and the Marriott hotels

The Moscone Center has a 200,000-sq-ft (186,000-sq-m) glass-enclosed expansion at 3rd and Howard Streets, which cost $551 million to build. It is an architectural highlight of the South of Market district.

TOP 10 ⭐ The Wine Country

The world-famous Wine Country comprises two picturesque valleys, Napa and Sonoma, the hills and dales surrounding them, and over 400 wineries. Napa is more developed for visitors, while Sonoma is more low-key but equally inviting. The area is fast recovering from the devastating 2017 wildfires, with nearly every winery, restaurant, and spa open for business *(see pp38–9)*.

1 Napa Valley Wine Train

Leaving from Napa and arriving in St. Helena, or vice versa, you can avoid the traffic and partake of a gourmet meal complemented by local wines. The trip takes 3 hours in total and the train **(below)** features a 1915 Pullman dining car.

2 Sterling Vineyards

There's a good self-guided tour at this mountain-top vineyard.

3 Beringer Vineyards

The oldest and the most beautiful Napa Valley winery **(below)**, established in 1876. Tours include a visit to the 1,000-ft (300-m) wine tunnels, which Chinese laborers carved out of volcanic stone.

4 Clos Pegase

Housed in an award-winning Post-Modern structure, this beguiling winery offers free tours and features an extensive collection of modern art. The wine is memorable, too – specialties include Cabernet, Merlot, and Portico port.

5 Yountville

Hot-air balloons float in the sky over the village of Yountville, where sweet cottages share the tree-lined streets with restaurants, galleries, upscale hotels, and V Marketplace, a gigantic brick edifice that houses shops, cafés, a spa, and wine-tasting salons.

Map of the Wine Country

6 The Culinary Institute of America

An impressive castle-like landmark, built in about 1890, houses the West Coast annex of the Culinary Institute of America. Foodies can stock up at the gourmet store, peruse the museum, or enjoy cookery and wine classes. The restaurant, with a terrace overlooking the vineyard, serves regional cuisine paired with appropriate wines.

7 Sonoma

This appealing town, nestled in the Valley of the Moon **(below)**, is filled with high-end restaurants, small hotels, and shops. The town also features a State Historic Park with a mission building and structures dating from the early to mid-1800s.

CALIFORNIA WINE

Since 1857, wine-making has been the main-stay of this area. A phylloxera blight in the early 1900s nearly put an end to it all, but Europe was hit harder, and it was the resistant California vines that brought back the wine business to parts of Italy, France, and Spain. In 1976 California wines were put on the international map, when they trounced France in a blind taste-test in Paris. These days, many European producers also have wineries in California.

8 Domaine Chandon

Lovely gardens, a fine restaurant, and sweeping views complement the sparkling, champagne-style wines of this Moët Hennessy showcase, which produces 500,000 cases every year.

9 Castello di Amorosa

This re-creation of a Medieval castle has a moat and a draw-bridge as well as a torture chamber. Take a guided tour and taste V. Sattui wines, which are produced here.

10 Hess Collection

The tours here are a pleasure, includ-ing not only wine-making facilities but also the owner's gallery of contemporary European and American artists. The Cabernet Sauvignon, Merlot, and Chardonnay **(right)** are all very good.

NEED TO KNOW

Napa Valley Wine Train:
1275 McKinstry St, Napa
■ (707) 253-2111
■ www.winetrain.com

Sterling Vineyards:
1111 Dunaweal Lane
■ (800) 726-6136 ■ www.sterlingvineyards.com

Beringer Vineyards:
2000 Main St, St. Helena
■ (707) 257-5771
■ www.beringer.com

Clos Pegase:
1060 Dunaweal Lane
■ (707) 942-4981
■ www.clospegase.com

The Culinary Institute of America: 2555 Main St, St. Helena
■ (707) 967-1100
■ www.ciachef.edu

Domaine Chandon:
1 California Drive, Yountville
■ (888) 242-6366
■ www.chandon.com

Castello di Amorosa:
4045 St. Helena Hwy, Calistoga ■ (707) 967-6272 ■ www.castellodiamorosa.com

Hess Collection:
4411 Redwood Rd, Napa
■ (707) 255-1144
■ www.hesscollection.com

■ For very special snacks, try the Model Bakery at 1357 Main St in St. Helena.

Wine Country Spas

1 Fairmont Sonoma Mission Inn & Spa

100 Boyes Blvd, Boyes Hot Springs ▪ (707) 938-9000 ▪ www.fairmont.com/sonoma

This famous inn provides an oasis of ultimate indulgence in luxury and refinement. Blessed by natural mineral hot springs, the legendary spa, with inspired architecture and lovely landscaping, exudes understated opulence and serenity.

Fairmont Sonoma Mission Inn & Spa

2 Indian Springs Calistoga

1712 Lincoln Ave, Calistoga ▪ (707) 942-4913 ▪ www.indian springscalistoga.com

Dating from 1862, this hot springs resort with mineral waters from natural geysers has been modernized but has an old-fashioned air about it, with an Olympic-sized heated pool, extensive gardens, and professional spa and mud bath treatments. On-site are lodge rooms and pretty cottages with fireplaces, kitchens, and air-conditioning. There's also a casual eatery and bar.

3 Health Spa Napa Valley

1030 Main St, St. Helena ▪ (707) 967-8800 ▪ www.napa valleyspa.com

In a serene, open-air setting, guests can yield aches and anxiety to a plethora of pampering and invigorating rituals. For some, that may mean a stimulating fitness workout, or a soothing mud wrap and massage overlooking the tranquil Spa Garden.

4 The Kenwood Inn and Spa

10400 Sonoma Hwy, Kenwood ▪ (707) 833-1293 ▪ www.kenwoodinn.com

Nationally acclaimed as one of the Wine Country's most elegant and intimate country inns, the Kenwood consists of lovely guest suites and a full-service spa facility. The inn has the ambience of an Italian country villa in the Sonoma Valley, situated on a secluded hillside facing over 1.5 sq miles (4 sq km) of vineyards. The spa offers a variety of massage styles, including aromatherapy and Ayurvedic.

5 Calistoga Spa Hot Springs

1006 Washington St, Calistoga ▪ (707) 942-6269 ▪ www.calistogaspa.com

Just off the main street, soak in the four outdoor geothermal mineral pools (with a wading pool for kids). Try a mud bath, use the gym, or take a yoga or Pilates class. Accommodations include contemporary rooms with kitchenettes.

6 Mount View Hotel & Spa

1457 Lincoln Ave, Calistoga ▪ (707) 942-6877 ▪ www.mount viewhotel.com

A stay in this historic 1917 resort offers various relaxation and rejuvenation possibilities – mud, milk, or herbal baths, aromatherapy steam showers, body wraps, massages, or facials – geared to individuals or couples.

7 Meritage Resort and Spa
875 Bordeaux Way, Napa ■ **(844) 283-4588** ■ **www.meritageresort.com**

Silence and serenity abide in this luxury resort. The stone-walled, Old World-style "Estate Cave" contains 12 treatment rooms, with whirlpools and saunas. The four-star hotel rooms are spacious; ask about the special packages on offer. On site, you will find restaurants, a large fitness studio, and a sports bar.

Meritage Resort and Spa

8 Silverado Resort and Spa
1600 Atlas Peak Rd, Napa ■ **(707) 257-0200** ■ **www.silveradoresort.com**

On 2 sq miles (5 sq km), studded by oak trees and anchored by a historic mansion housing restaurants and lounges, this luxury resort in the Wine Country has two championship golf courses, dozens of swimming pools, and a tennis complex. The upscale spa offers 12 rooms for top-notch body treatments, plus private garden pavilions, a nail and hair salon, a café, yoga classes, and workout facilities.

9 Villagio Inn and Spa
6481 Washington St, Yountville ■ **(707) 944-8877** ■ **www.villagio.com**

Fireplaces, water features, and lush gardens create rustic luxury, to be enjoyed in the 16 treatment rooms with Swiss showers, saunas, and secluded outdoor baths. Spa suites for couples are romantic enclosures with soaking tubs, fireplaces, steam showers, and private terraces. At the associated four-star Villagio Inn, spacious rooms are surrounded by gardens adorned with replicas of Greek and Roman statuary.

10 Boon Hotel + Spa
14711 Armstrong Woods Rd, Guerneville ■ **(707) 869-2721** ■ **www.boonhotels.com**

In the beautiful redwoods of the Russian River area, this small, peaceful, adults-only inn offers an invigorating retreat from modern life. Body treatments include deep-tissue massages, hot-stone massages, and soothing facials with seaweed anti-wrinkle masks. Included in your stay are use of the pool and Jacuzzi, and evening wine-tastings on selected weekends. The restaurant serves Russian River wines, and sources ingredients from local suppliers or from its garden.

Championship golf course at Silverado Resort and Spa

The Top 10 of Everything

Interior of Grace Cathedral

🔟 Moments in History

Depiction of Native American hunters in San Francisco Bay

1 Native Americans

There were settlements in the Bay as early as the 11th century BC, made up of hunters and gatherers who enjoyed a rich diet of seeds, shellfish, and game. Historians group these peoples into the Coast Miwok, the Wintun, and the Ohlone.

2 Sir Francis Drake

In 1579, the English privateer landed near Point Reyes and claimed Alta California for Queen Elizabeth I. Along with other early explorers of the area, he failed to notice the marvelous Bay just inside the straits. England didn't follow up its claim to Northern California, leaving it to the Spanish to conquer.

Drawing of gold seekers landing in San Francisco, 1849

3 Spanish Control

About 200 years after Drake's wanderings, Spain got serious about establishing a presence in Alta California. In 1776, an expedition led by Juan Bautista de Anza arrived at San Francisco Bay and established the Presidio (fort). A mission was also founded by Father Junípero Serra (see p108).

4 American Takeover

Impending war with Mexico in the 1840s inspired US leaders to arouse the interest of Bay Area settlers in joining the Union. In 1846, a party of Yankees in Sonoma declared California's independence from Mexico, christening it the Bear Flag Republic. Shortly after, Commodore John Sloat claimed California as US territory.

5 Gold Rush Days

In 1848 landowner John Sutter noticed a curious glitter in the sediment of the American River in the Sierra Nevada foothills and realized it was gold. Despite attempts to keep the discovery quiet, word leaked out, and businessman Sam Brannan displayed a bottle of gold dust and nuggets for the whole city to see. The subsequent stampede of prospectors, dubbed the '49ers, made the city a boomtown overnight.

Wells Fargo
Located in the bank's headquarters, at 420 Montgomery Street, the Wells Fargo Museum displays the rollicking stagecoaches of the 1850s that carried freight and fortune-seekers to the city during the Gold Rush *(see p53)*.

Panama-Pacific Exposition
Held in 1915 to celebrate the opening of the Panama Canal, the real *raison d'être* for the festivities was that San Franciscans had resurrected their city after the 1906 disaster.

Bay and Golden Gate Bridges
The inauguration of the Bay Bridge in 1936 heralded the end of the age of ferryboats by linking the city to the East Bay. The inauguration of the Golden Gate Bridge *(see pp12–13)* took place a year later.

"Summer of Love"
San Francisco counterculture burst forth in the summer of 1967. Hippies were everywhere, and the poetic music that embodied a new way of thinking filled the air. It was a sociopolitical shift that went on to affect the whole world.

Modern Politics
California has always been a few steps ahead of the rest of the United States. In 1992, it became the first state to send two female Senators, Dianne Feinstein and Barbara Boxer, to the US Congress, while Nancy Pelosi was the first ever female Speaker of the House of Representatives from 2007 to 2011.

Dianne Feinstein

TOP 10 SCANDALS AND DISASTERS

The ruins of the 1906 earthquake

1 Native Americans' Near-Extinction
In the late 1800s, Native Americans were hunted down by settlers, with a bounty paid for each scalp.

2 Gold Rush Lawlessness
Gold Rush frontier life was so criminal that vigilante justice was proclaimed in the 1850s, leading to secret trials.

3 1906
An earthquake and consequent fire devastated much of the city, and 250,000 people were left homeless.

4 "Bloody Thursday"
On July 5, 1934, the police fired shots at longshoremen who were on strike, leaving two of them dead.

5 Howl
On October 13, 1955, Allen Ginsberg read his revolutionary poem, which was later banned as obscene, at the Six Gallery in San Francisco.

6 Freedom and Anti-War Riots
Pro-Civil Rights and anti-Vietnam War riots occurred from 1964 to 1970.

7 Death of a Rock Icon
Part of hippie legend, Janis Joplin died of a heroin overdose in 1970.

8 White's Revenge
In 1978 ex-Supervisor Dan White shot dead Mayor George Moscone and gay Supervisor Harvey Milk *(see p47)*. He was controversially convicted of manslaughter rather than murder.

9 AIDS
The epidemic reached overwhelming proportions in the city in the 1980s.

10 Loma Prieta Earthquake
In October 1989, the quake destroyed the Victorian center of Santa Cruz *(see p65)* and part of the Bay Bridge.

ᴛᴏᴘ10 Writers and Notable Residents

"Beat" author Jack Kerouac

1 Jack Kerouac
Arriving from New York in 1947, it was Kerouac (1922–69) who coined the term "Beat." He and his companions – Neal Cassady, Allen Ginsberg, Lawrence Ferlinghetti, and others – initiated the new politics of dissent and free love that led, within a decade, to the hippie movement *(see p43)*. His novel *On the Road* (1957) galvanized a generation.

2 Isabel Allende
One of the world's most widely read Spanish-language authors, this Chilean-American Bay Area resident is famous for her magic realism in *The House of the Spirits*, *City of the Beasts*, *Eva Luna*, and *Of Love and Shadows*. She received the Presidential Medal of Freedom in 2014.

3 Robin Williams
A resident of the Bay Area from when he was a teenager, TV and movie star Williams (1951–2014) began his career as a stand-up comedian in San Francisco clubs and was credited with kick-starting the comedy "renaissance" of the 1970s. Beloved by and friendly to locals, he was known for his generosity to Bay Area charities.

4 William Randolph Hearst
A flamboyant publisher of the *San Francisco Examiner* who built the nation's largest newspaper chain in the late 1800s, Hearst (1863–1951) influenced the American press with his "yellow journalism" tactics, built Hearst Castle, served twice in the House of Representatives, and inspired the movie *Citizen Kane*.

5 Francis Ford Coppola
The director of *The Godfather* makes San Francisco the home of his American Zoetrope productions, and has also branched out into other enterprises. His Inglenook winery in the Napa Valley is one of the best.

6 Jack London
Adventurer and author of frontier tales such as *White Fang*, *The Sea Wolf*, and *The Call of the Wild*, Jack London (1876–1916) grew up in Oakland. A museum of his memorabilia is now housed there, in a reconstruction of the log cabin he lived in while prospecting for gold in the Yukon territory. His fiction is based on his experiences in the untamed West and the social inequality he saw in boomtown San Francisco.

Jack London statue

7 Dashiell Hammett
The author of *The Maltese Falcon* and creator of the classic hard-boiled detective Sam Spade lived in San Francisco from 1921 to 1929. He used the fog-swirled slopes of the hills as the backdrop for his crime stories. Hammett (1894–1961) was himself employed briefly at the famous Pinkerton Detective Agency.

Armistead Maupin

Maupin's *Tales of the City* were serialized in the *San Francisco Chronicle* before being published in book form. They are lighthearted paeans to the idiosyncrasies of gay San Francisco in the 1970s, before AIDS changed everything.

Carlos Santana

A Mexican-American who grew up in San Francisco and was influenced by Bay Area 1960s jazz and folk musicians, Santana founded a band that pioneered Afro-Latin-blues-rock fusion at the Fillmore West, in other area clubs, and at Woodstock. He went on to top the *Billboard* charts for decades, selling more than 100 million records.

Carlos Santana in concert

Joe DiMaggio

DiMaggio (1914–99) was born and began his baseball career in San Francisco. His 56-game hitting streak with the New York Yankees made him a legend. He married Marilyn Monroe in San Francisco.

Baseball player Joe DiMaggio

TOP 10 SIXTIES FIGURES

Janis Joplin

1 Janis Joplin
This troubled singer from Texas was the queen of the San Francisco sound, until her death by heroin overdose.

2 Ken Kesey
A powerful, revolutionary writer, his Magic Bus and Trips Festival set the tone for the entire hippie movement.

3 Jerry Garcia
Patriarch of the San Francisco sound, his Grateful Dead band continued to tour until his death in 1995.

4 Mario Savio
The UC Berkeley student launched the Free Speech Movement on the campus in the late 1960s.

5 Owsley Stanley
Stanley manufactured mass quantities of LSD and was the most famous source of pure LSD in the 1960s.

6 Grace Slick
A quintessentially San Franciscan voice, Slick fronted Jefferson Airplane.

7 Huey Newton
Oakland's founder of the Black Panthers, a group committed to change, by violence if necessary.

8 Patty Hearst
The newspaper heiress, kidnapped by the Symbionese Liberation Army in 1974, was apparently converted and took part in an armed robbery.

9 Jim Jones
Leader of a cult that moved en masse to South America. He ended his days and those of some 900 followers in 1978, in a mass suicide caused by drinking cyanide-laced Kool-Aid.

10 Charles Manson
This commune leader and his followers murdered actress Sharon Tate in 1969.

 Historic Sites

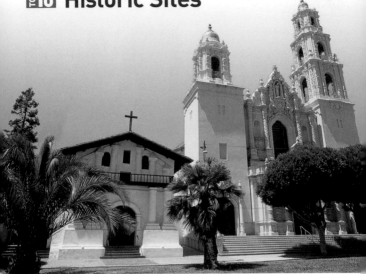

Facades of the chapel and basilica, Mission Dolores

1 Mission Dolores
This 18th-century Spanish mission is the oldest building in the city. Its 4 ft (1.2 m) thick adobe walls and red-tile roofs are typical of the "Mission Style" seen all over California (see p109).

2 Jackson Square
This area contains some of the city's oldest, loveliest buildings (see p88). One of the few places spared in the 1906 conflagration.

3 Nob Hill
Home to historic hotels and remnants of the golden age of the railroad barons. The Fairmont Hotel (1907) is famous for the Tonga Room & Hurricane Bar, and the Mark Hopkins (1939) is crowned by the Top of the Mark lounge. Grace Cathedral's towers loom over all (see p87).

4 The Presidio
More than 350 buildings, which spent 200 years in a military enclave, have been repurposed as museums, restaurants, and recreational facilities. Highlights are a National Cemetery, Civil War barracks, Victorian mansions, a World War II memorial, the Walt Disney Family Museum, the Society of California Pioneers Museum, and the heritage gallery in the Officers' Club (see pp98–9).

5 War Memorial Opera House
Inaugurated in 1932, this building is dedicated to World War I soldiers. In 1945 it hosted the plenary sessions that preceded the founding of the UN and, in 1951, it was the site of the signing of the peace treaty between the US and Japan (see p68).

Huntington Park Fountain, Nob Hill

6 North Beach

This entire area resonates with the history of the early Italian residents, but even more with the iconoclastic legacy of the revolutionary Beats, who brought the neighborhood worldwide fame. Historic churches stand as clear landmarks, while equally historic saloons and cafés take a little snooping around to find (see p87).

7 Haight-Ashbury

The matrix of yet another bohemian movement that San Francisco has given birth to, this area nurtured idealistic hippies in the late 1960s. They brought international awareness to alternative ways of life, living in harmony with nature (see p104).

8 Fillmore Auditorium

MAP E3 ▪ 1805 Geary Blvd

One of the legendary homes of psychedelic rock during the 1960s. Along with the Avalon Ballroom and the Winterland (both now gone), this is where the San Francisco sound found its first audience.

9 Ferry Building Marketplace

Once the tallest building in the city, with a 235-ft- (71.6-m-) high clock tower modeled after the Giralda tower in Seville, in 1898 this was the headquarters of countless streetcars and ferryboats. Fireboat crews saved the tower from the 1906 fire. Now, it's a huge food hall and marketplace (see p78).

10 Fort Point National Historic Site

MAP C1 ▪ Marine Drive

At this much-photographed site under the Golden Gate Bridge, swords, guns, and cannons are on view at a fortification that was built during the Civil War to protect the city from an attack by sea, which never came. Rangers and costumed docents give free tours of the gunpowder storehouse, the barracks, and the museum.

TOP 10 HISTORIC FIGURES

John Muir

1 John Muir
A keen promoter of the National Parks movement. The Muir Woods are named in his honor (see p64).

2 John C. Fremont
Instrumental in the US annexation of California in the mid-1800s, it was Fremont who dubbed the Bay strait the "Golden Gate."

3 Junípero Serra
This 18th-century Spanish cleric traveled up and down California establishing missions, including Mission Dolores (see p109).

4 Leland Stanford
One of the "Big Four" who masterminded the Transcontinental Railroad, he also founded Stanford University (see p126).

5 Mark Hopkins
Another of the "Big Four" who became super-rich and lived on Nob Hill.

6 Charles Crocker
The Crocker Galleria recalls the legacy of this "Big Four" member (see p78).

7 A. P. Giannini
Founder in 1904 of the Bank of Italy, later the Bank of America, Giannini financed the Golden Gate Bridge.

8 Harvey Milk
The first openly gay politician to become a member of the Board of Supervisors was assassinated in 1978.

9 Dianne Feinstein
One of the movers and shakers of San Francisco politics in recent decades, she became a US Senator in 1992.

10 Jerry Brown
The first three-term Governor of California and former Mayor of Oakland also ran for US President.

TOP 10 Churches

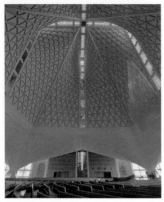

Cathedral of St. Mary of the Assumption

1 Cathedral of St. Mary of the Assumption

MAP F3 ▪ 1111 Gough St ▪ (415) 567-2020 ▪ Services: 6:45am, 8am & 12:10pm Mon–Fri; 6:45am, 8am & 5:30pm Sat; 7:30am, 9am, 11am & 1pm (Spanish) Sun ▪ www.st marycathedralsf.org

The exterior of this 1971 building has been compared to a giant washing machine; inside is equally odd, with stained-glass strips meeting to form a colorful cross (see p50).

2 Grace Cathedral

The Notre Dame of San Francisco mixes Italian Renaissance with Gothic architecture and a lot of American originality (see p87).

3 St. Mark's Lutheran Church

MAP P1 ▪ 1111 O'Farrell St ▪ (415) 928-7770 ▪ Services: 9am & 11am Sun ▪ www.sfmarks-sf.org

This 1895 pink-brick church is a mixture of Gothic and Romanesque styles. After the 1906 earthquake (see p43), it served as a first-aid station and shelter.

4 Mission Dolores

Photos and a diorama offer a stirring impression of what life was like for the Ohlone people – Native Americans – who built this Spanish mission in the 18th century (see p109).

5 St. Patrick's Cathedral

MAP Q4 ▪ 756 Mission St ▪ (415) 421-3730 ▪ Services: 7:30am, 12:10pm & 5:15pm Mon–Sat; 7:30am, 9am, 10:30am, 12:15pm & 5:15pm Sun ▪ www.stpatricksf.org

Constructed in 1872, this Gothic Revival cathedral has an impressive marble and stained-glass interior.

6 Glide Memorial United Methodist Church

MAP Q3 ▪ 330 Ellis St ▪ (415) 674-6000 ▪ Services: 9am & 11am Sun ▪ www.glide.org

This church has a credo of "the human condition first, not the Bible." Services can draw up to 1,500 celebrants, with a gospel choir. Same-sex couples can exchange vows of matrimony in this institution.

7 Saints Peter and Paul Church

North Beach's "Italian Cathedral" was once called the "Marzipan Church" for the stucco decoration on its soaring pinnacles (see p92). Inside, there is a sculpted reproduction of Leonardo da Vinci's *Last Supper*.

Stained glass, Saints Peter and Paul Chur

8 Shrine of St. Francis of Assisi

MAP M4 ▪ 610 Vallejo St at Columbus ▪ (415) 986-4557 ▪ Services: 12:15pm Mon–Sat, 11am Sun ▪ www.shrinesf.org

Declared a National Historic Landmark, the Gothic Revival St. Francis of Assisi Church was established on June 17, 1849, as the first parish church in California. The interior is adorned with 11 larger-than-life murals, depicting the works of San Francisco's patron saint.

Art by Mark Dukes, St. John Coltrane African Orthodox Church

9 St. John Coltrane African Orthodox Church

MAP F3 ▪ St. Paul's Lutheran Church, 1286 Fillmore St ▪ (415) 673-7144 ▪ Services: noon Sun ▪ www.coltrane church.org

"My music is the spiritual expression of what I am" said the jazz musician St. John Coltrane. Services consist of a performance of his *A Love Supreme* by the band Ohnedaruth and the Sisters of Compassion choir.

10 First Unitarian Universalist Church

MAP P1 ▪ 1187 Franklin St ▪ (415) 776-4580 ▪ Services: 11am Sun ▪ www.uusf.org

Since 1850, this church has been a progressive voice in San Francisco. Welcoming all faiths and creeds, this congregation is not bound by dogma, but by shared values.

TOP 10 OTHER PLACES OF WORSHIP

Exterior of Kong Chow Temple

1 Kong Chow Temple
Chinatown's oldest temple is dedicated to Guan Di, a male deity.

2 Tin How Temple
The Queen of Heaven rules this sanctuary and makes sure devotees travel safely by water, among other things *(see p62)*.

3 Congregation Sherith Israel
MAP F3 ▪ 2266 California St ▪ Services: 6pm Fri, 9:15am Sat ▪ sherithisrael.org
Founded in 1849 by Jewish pioneers, the domed synagogue dates from 1904.

4 Vedanta Temple
MAP M5 ▪ 2323 Vallejo St ▪ sfvedanta.org
This was the first Hindu temple (1905) in the western US.

5 Zen Center
MAP F4 ▪ 300 Page St ▪ sfzc.org
Home to the city's Zen practitioners.

6 Crystal Way
MAP F5 ▪ 2335 Market St
Healing through crystals, light, sound, and positive thinking are explored.

7 Shambhala Meditation Center
MAP F4 ▪ 1231 Stevenson St ▪ www.shambhala.org
Meditations, talks and classes take place here.

8 Spirit Rock Meditation Center
5000 Sir Francis Drake Blvd, Woodacre ▪ www.spiritrock.org
This center helps people find peace through meditation.

9 The Love of Ganesha
MAP E4 ▪ 1573 Haight St
Hindu clothing, arts, and crafts.

10 Open Secret
923 C St, San Rafael ▪ www.opensecretbookstore.com
The backroom of this New Age venue is like a temple to all the world's deities.

📟 **Architectural Highlights**

Staircase of City Hall, Civic Center

1 Civic Center

This complex is centered on City Hall, a Baroque Revival paragon (1915) with a golden dome, attracting tourists and wedding parties for photos on its curving marble staircase decorated with filigree iron and gilt. The other buildings are in Beaux Arts style. Befitting the city that started the Gold Rush, gilt is everywhere *(see p89)*.

2 Transamerica Pyramid
MAP N5 ■ 600 Montgomery St

A sparkling white obelisk made out of crushed quartz, the pyramid is an iconic symbol of the city. At 853 ft (260 m), it is the second tallest building in San Francisco. At its base is Redwood Park, where office workers relax on weekdays. Shop for souvenirs and exhibits in the lobby.

3 555 California Street
MAP N5 ■ 555 California St

This 52-story structure, known previously as the Bank of America Center, was the first skyscraper to be erected in the city, in 1972. The color was a mistake – the granite that faces it was supposed to be pink, not brown, but by the time the delivery was made, it was too late to change it.

4 San Francisco Museum of Modern Art

This striking post-modern oculus was designed by architect Mario Botta. It was augmented by the Norwegian firm, Snøhetta, with a rippling facade replicating the waters and fog of San Francisco Bay *(see pp32–3)*.

5 Palace of Fine Arts
MAP E1 ■ 3301 Lyon St ■ (415) 563-6504 ■ www.palaceoffinearts.org

This Neo-Classical building, today used for shows, was designed by Bernard Maybeck for the Pan-Pacific Exposition of 1915 and inspired by the engravings of Giovanni Piranesi.

6 Cathedral of St. Mary of the Assumption

Some critics dismiss this parabolic form, but the soaring curves take attention upward, in the same way that tracery and vaulting do in Gothic cathedrals *(see p48)*.

7 Coit Tower

Perched on Telegraph Hill, this Art Deco sentinel takes the form of a giant fluted column. Reminiscent of Renaissance towers, the column is 210 ft (64 m) tall and is perforated

Coit Tower, Telegraph Hill

around the top with arched openings and windows, which visitors can reach by elevator for stunning views of the city. Depression-era murals decorate the lobby (see p92).

8 Grace Cathedral

The third largest Episcopal church in the US was executed in the medieval French Gothic style. Its stained-glass windows glow atop Nob Hill (see p87).

Grace Cathedral

9 Haas-Lilienthal House

MAP M1 ▪ 2007 Franklin St ▪ (415) 441-3011 ▪ Open noon–3pm Sat & Wed, 11am–4pm Sun ▪ Adm ▪ www.sfheritage.org

This Queen Anne-style mansion, built in 1886, is one of the few Victorian beauties in the city that accepts visitors. It's a wonderful glimpse into the way of life among San Francisco's upper-middle classes from about 1890 to 1920. Gables, a turret, and fancy embellishments make this a showstopper on Franklin Street.

10 Alamo Square

MAP E4

With a downtown backdrop and a sweeping greensward below, these vividly hued late 1800s Victorian mansions (or "Painted Ladies") are on the 700 block of Steiner Street. The surrounding streets boast gems built between the 1870s and 1920s.

TOP 10 PUBLIC ART SITES

1 Balmy Alley
MAP G6 ▪ 24th & 25th Sts between Harrison & Treat
The most famous set of murals in town, by local Latino artists.

2 San Francisco Art Institute
MAP K3 ▪ 800 Chestnut St
Diego Rivera, the Mexican muralist, painted *The Making of a Fresco* here.

3 Day Lights
This installation of 25,000 LED lights on the Bay Bridge is the work of Leo Villareal.

4 Fort Mason
MAP J1 ▪ Franklin St
Oliver DiCicco's *Bow Seat* pays homage to small boats that have worked the Bay.

5 Women's Building
MAP F5 ▪ 18th St between Valencia & Guerrero
The work of seven women painters graces the facade.

6 Bikeway
MAP F4 ▪ Duboce St between Church & Market
This mural chronicles a bike ride from Downtown to Ocean Beach.

7 Golden Gate Park
The Music Concourse is home to many sculptures, including the bronze *Apple Cider Press* (see pp24–5).

8 Rincon Center
MAP H2 ▪ Mission, Howard, Steuart & Spear Sts
These 1948 murals by Russian Anton Refregier trace Californian history.

9 Financial District
The black-stone *Transcendence* is in front of 555 California Street.

10 Beach Chalet
MAP A4 ▪ 1000 Great Hwy
Depression-era murals depicting famous citizens of San Francisco.

Beach Chalet mural

🔟 Museums

1 de Young Museum

A bastion of American, Oceanian, and African art, the de Young is a landmark in Golden Gate Park, topped by a 144-ft (44-m) observation tower. Founded with pieces from the 1894 California Midwinter Fair, the Oceanic and African groupings have been expanded with private collections. There is a sculpture garden and a collection of American art from colonial times to the 20th century (see pp28–9).

2 California Academy of Sciences

The environmentally-friendly architecture of the Academy's building, which emphasizes ecological and sustainable features, blends with the natural surroundings of the park. The museum covers virtually every aspect of the natural world (see pp26–7).

3 Legion of Honor

This museum, located above Land's End, is set in a beautiful French Neo-Classical building, which was built to commemorate the soldiers from California who died in World War I. Four thousand years of ancient and European art are displayed here, ranging from a major Rodin collection, including

The Three Shades, **Legion of Honor**

The Three Shades, to works by Rubens, Rembrandt, Degas, and Monet. The museum also houses priceless antiquities from the ancient lands of Egypt, Greece, and Rome (see p117). Views of Lincoln Park are enjoyed from the café terrace.

4 Asian Art Museum

MAP R2 ■ 200 Larkin St
■ (415) 581-3500 ■ Open 10am–5pm Tue–Sun ■ Adm ■ www.asianart.org

Set in the old Main Library which was restructured by Italian architect, Gae Aulenti, the Asian Art Museum has been transformed into a dramatic contemporary home for a vast collection of Chinese, Korean, Japanese, Himalayan, and Southeast Asian works. On display is the fabulous Avery Brundage collection of Oriental jade, and Buddhist art from India to the Far

Korean costume, Asian Art Museum

East. Special exhibitions are regularly held here. Café Asia, which serves authentic cuisine from the region, is popular among local office workers.

⑤ San Francisco Museum of Modern Art

Located in the South of Market museum district, the SFMOMA features seven levels of 20th-century art, admission-free public areas, outdoor terraces, a café, a restaurant, and a large gift shop (see pp32–3).

⑥ San Francisco Museum of Craft and Design

MAP H5 ■ 2569 Third St ■ (415) 773-0303 ■ Open 11am–6pm Tue–Sat, noon–5pm Sun ■ Closed major public hols ■ Adm ■ www.sfmcd.org

This one-of-a-kind museum celebrates and promotes contemporary craft and design through innovative exhibitions and educational programs. Many lectures, special shows, and programs are organized to engage children, all designed to stimulate creativity. There is also a great museum store with many original, handmade pieces for sale.

⑦ Wells Fargo History Museum

MAP N5 ■ 420 Montgomery St ■ (415) 396-2619 ■ Open 9am–5pm Mon–Fri ■ www.wellsfargo history.com

Tales of the robbers who held up Wells Fargo stagecoaches (see p43) are the stuff of legend. Exhibits here include Pony Express mail, gold nuggets, and Emperor Norton's currency.

⑧ Society of California Pioneers

MAP D2 ■ 101 Montgomery St, Suite 150 ■ (415) 957-1849 ■ Open 10am–5pm Wed–Sat ■ www.californiapioneers.org

This museum displays a fascinating collection of historical exhibits from 19th- and 20th-century California. The upstairs gallery features an annually rotating exhibition of items from the private collection.

⑨ Contemporary Jewish Museum (CJM)

Across the street from Yerba Buena Gardens, this charming 1907 Willis Polk-designed power substation was adapted by architect Daniel Libeskind in 1998. His design was inspired by the Hebrew letters that spell *chai* (life), the *chet* and the *yud*. Soaring blue steel blocks front the plaza, which change color in different light as if they were alive. The small collection of contemporary and ancient Jewish artistic, historical, and cultural items is augmented by ever-changing exhibits encompassing political art, iconic Jewish figures, immigration, architecture, modern Israel, and more (see p35).

Contemporary Jewish Museum

⑩ Maritime Museum

MAP F1 ■ 900 Beach St, Aquatic Park ■ (415) 447-5000 ■ Open 9:30am–4pm daily ■ www.maritime.org

The 1939 bathhouse in which this museum is located was designed in the Streamline Moderne style, a late offshoot of the Art Deco period. Being modeled after the clean lines of an ocean liner, it looks for all the world like a cruise ship about to set sail into the Bay. Inside, it is awash with ship models, figureheads, maritime paintings, photos, and seagoing relics like scrimshaw, ships in bottles, and knot-tied folk art.

🔟 Art Galleries

1 City Art Gallery

MAP F5 ▪ 828 Valencia St between 19th & 20th ▪ (415) 970-9900 ▪ Open noon–9pm Wed–Sun ▪ www.cityartgallery.org

Owned and operated by the artists themselves, this cooperative gallery prides itself on making artwork accessible and affordable to those interested in collecting art. Showcasing the work of around 200 local artists – some new, some known and established – the gallery exhibits an array of styles and media through changing exhibitions. Eighty percent of any sale goes directly to the artist.

2 Gallery Wendi Norris

MAP P3 ▪ 161 Jessie St ▪ (415) 346-7812 ▪ Open 11am–6pm Tue–Sat ▪ www.gallerywendinorris.com

This dynamic and extremely stylish contemporary art venue in South of Market hosts exhibitions of celebrated American and international works, including those by prominent artists from China, Japan, South Korea, and Russia. Some Bay Area artists are also featured in the gallery. The staff is on hand to provide advice to amateur and serious collectors alike about the contemporary art market.

3 Pacific Heritage Museum

MAP N5 ▪ 608 Commercial St ▪ (415) 399-1124 ▪ Open 10am–4pm Tue–Sat

Occupying the historic US Sub-Treasury building from 1875, on top of which the East West Bank has been built. The bank sponsors the museum, which focuses on the art of the Pacific Rim, aiming to bring the work of Asian artists to a wider audience. Exhibitions feature many pieces on loan from private collections.

4 SOMArts Cultural Center

MAP G4 ▪ 934 Brannan St between 8th & 9th Sts ▪ (415) 863-1414 ▪ Open noon–7pm Tue–Fri, noon–5pm Sat ▪ www.somarts.org

Group and solo shows, music, and readings all take place here. Founded in 1975, SOMArts is a city-owned cultural center with two exhibition spaces, a 250-seat theater, and printmaking, photography, and design studios.

5 Fraenkel Gallery

MAP P4 ▪ 49 Geary St ▪ (415) 981-2661 ▪ Open 10:30am–5:30pm Tue–Fri, 11am–5pm Sat ▪ www.fraenkelgallery.com

Opened in 1979, the gallery held an exhibition early on of NASA's lunar photographs, and this set the tone for what followed. Soon came exhibitions by Eugene Atget, Edward Weston, Hiroshi Sugimoto, and Diane Arbus, and later, the Bechers, Adam Fuss, and Sol LeWitt. Projects have brought together work across all

Fraenkel Gallery

media, juxtaposing photography with painting, drawing, and sculpture. Other photographers whose work is regularly shown include Richard Avedon and Man Ray.

Intersection for the Arts

6 Intersection for the Arts
MAP G3 ■ 925 Mission St at 5th St ■ (415) 626-2787 ■ Hours vary, call ahead ■ www.theintersection.org
Radical and diverse art emerges from this hotbed of creativity. The alternative multi-genre art installation combines drama, video and film screenings, and panel discussions exploring the influence of race and relationships on people's work and lives.

7 Museo Italo Americano
MAP F1 ■ Fort Mason Center, Bldg C ■ (415) 673-2200 ■ Open noon–4pm daily (Mon by appointment only) ■ www.museoitalo americano.org
A museum, gallery, and community center for San Francisco's Italians. Regular changing temporary exhibitions might focus on the work of either an individual Italian artist, or on aspects of Italian culture. Classes are also offered at the center on Italian art history, culture, architecture, and cookery.

8 Galería de la Raza
MAP G5 ■ 2857 24th St ■ (415) 826-8009 ■ Open noon–6pm Wed–Sat, noon–5pm Sun ■ www.galeriadelaraza.org
This gallery promotes awareness and appreciation of Latino/Chicano art including painting, photography, and sculpture. Galeria de la Raza also provides a platform for the performing arts, spoken word nights, as well as projecting digital murals on the building's facade.

9 John Berggruen Gallery
MAP P4 ■ 228 Grant Ave ■ (415) 781-4629 ■ Open 9:30am–5:30pm Mon–Fri, 10:30am–5pm Sat ■ www.berggruen.com
One of the most popular galleries for the exhibition and sale of modern American and European art since the 70s. Their displays have included artworks from masters such as de Kooning, Calder, and Matisse.

10 San Francisco Arts Commission Gallery
MAP R1 ■ 401 Van Ness Ave ■ (415) 554-6080 ■ Open noon–5pm Wed–Sat ■ www.sfartscommission.org/gallery
Opened in 1970, this was one of the first galleries dedicated to showing the work of emerging Bay Area artists. In addition, the Gallery Slide Registry contains images by more than 500 professional artists from across the US.

Parks and Gardens

1 Marina Green
MAP E1

Within sight of the Golden Gate Bridge, and across the street from photogenic 1930s mansions and the Palace of Fine Arts, are several blocks of bayside greensward, which are perfect for picnicking and people-watching. On weekends, observe kite-flyers, joggers, and cyclists, as well as yoga, tai chi, and Zumba practitioners. Some people work out on the seven-station fitness circuit.

2 Alta Plaza
MAP E2

This double block of verdant hill in Pacific Heights is a popular place to sit in the sun when it ventures to break through the fog. Basketball and tennis courts and a children's playground are in the center, while to the south there are terraced lawns, onto which face some of the oldest homes in Pacific Heights.

3 Fort Mason
MAP F1

The rolling lawn above Fort Mason Center (see p99), known as the Great Meadow, is a relatively little-used park, but it's great for taking a siesta, tossing a frisbee, or just strolling through to take in the spectacular views from the cliffs.

4 The Presidio
This vast swath of greenery only entered the city's parklands in 1994. It is a beautiful space, and tourists and locals alike come to enjoy the wooded areas, walking trails, and wonderful views over the Bay (see pp98–9). It is also home to chic restaurants and museums (see p46). Filmmaker George Lucas created a $350 million headquarters here for his production company Lucasfilm with up to 1,500 employees.

The Victorian Conservatory of Flowers, Golden Gate Park

5 Conservatory of Flowers
Shipped around Cape Horn from England and erected in Golden Gate Park in 1879, this magnificent five-story Victorian greenhouse contains a jungle of trees, palms, exotic plants, and flowers (see p24). There are thousands of orchids, an enchanting butterfly enclosure, and lily ponds. Plant lovers come from around the world to learn about endangered flora and horticultural innovations like aquascaping.

The Presidio

6 Golden Gate Park

One of the largest city parks in the US is also one of the most diverse, and all of it was brought forth from what was once scrub and dunes. The park also features first-rate cultural attractions such as the de Young Museum (see pp28–9).

7 Lafayette Park
MAP F2

This is another of the double-blocked hilltop gardens in Pacific Heights – a leafy green haven of pine and eucalyptus trees. Steep stairways lead to the summit of the park, which has delightful views.

8 Rincon Park
MAP H2

Situated just south of the Ferry Building Marketplace on the Embarcadero pedestrian prome-nade, Cupid's Span, a 60-ft- (18-m-) tall sculpture of a red-feathered bow and arrow, marks the location of this bayside park. The lawns and benches afford awesome views of the San Francisco–Oakland Bay Bridge, the city skyline, and passing ships.

9 Yerba Buena Gardens

In the South of Market museum district, surrounding the Yerba Buena Center for the Arts, are lawns, shade trees,

Esplanade at the Yerba Buena Gardens

gardens, and water features, which create a verdant setting for whimsical outdoor sculptures. Don't miss the 50-ft- (15-m-) wide Martin Luther King, Jr. waterfall (see pp34–5).

10 Sigmund Stern Recreation Grove
Hwy 1 & Sloat Blvd

Famous for its free summer concerts, Sigmund Stern Recreation Grove is a leafy recreation complex con-taining playing fields, tennis and croquet courts, as well as a play-ground, and a dog park. Pine Lake is popular for jogging, and there are plenty of good picnic spots under the eucalyptus, redwood, and pine trees.

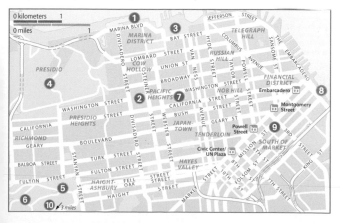

TOP 10 Beaches

Popular sands of Stinson Beach

1 Stinson Beach

Three miles (5 km) of sand, coupled with the fact that Marin County often has fine weather when the rest of the coast is covered in fog, make this one of the most popular beaches in the Bay Area. It can be busy when it's sunny *(see pp126–7)*.

2 Muir and Red Rock Beaches

Muir Beach: off Hwy 1 on Pacific Way ■ **Red Rock: 5.5 miles (9 km) north of Muir on Pacific Way**

These two beaches, just south of Stinson, are the most famous nude beaches north of San Francisco. Both are sandy curves within their own coves, protected from wind and prying eyes by rocky cliffs. The only caveat is that you'll need sturdy

The cliffs overlooking Muir Beach

walking shoes to get down the rough paths that lead to them from the parking lots.

3 China Beach
MAP B2

This is the poshest beach in San Francisco, being adjacent to the exclusive Sea Cliff neighborhood. Despite its pedigree, California law requires that all coastal areas remain public, although access roads to them can be private. China Beach is small and protected from the wind, there's plenty of parking, and it's a pleasant walk to the sand. You'll find showers and changing rooms, as well as grills and picnic areas here.

4 Pacifica Beaches
Hwy 1

A 20-minute drive south of the city are several Pacific Ocean beaches popular with surfers, swimmers, and families. A favorite of beginner surfers, Linda Mar Beach has rest-rooms and showers, and connects by a breezy trail to Rockaway Beach. Sharp Park Beach has picnic sites, a fishing pier with a café, parking, and nature trails.

5 Bolinas Beach

This hidden-away Marin beach tends to be windy and is mostly used by dog-walkers and kayakers *(see p127)*. It's sandy, with a backdrop of rocky cliffs. If you walk north, you'll find sheltered nooks, where some sun-worshippers bask in the nude, although there is a rarely enforced city ordinance against it.

The Golden Gate Bridge viewed from Baker Beach

6 Baker Beach
MAP C2

This 1-mile (1.5-km) stretch of sandy beach, with its perfect views of the Golden Gate Bridge, is the most popular in the city. It's great for sunbathing, dog-walking, picnicking, or jogging, but signs warn off swimmers because of riptides. The sunsets here are unforgettable.

7 Ocean Beach

Some 4 miles (6.5 km) long and quite broad, this is the city's largest beach by far, but probably the worst for entering the water safely. It starts at Cliff House and continues on beyond the city limits, turning into picturesque dunes at the southern end. Great for walking or jogging, and when the sun comes out, it's a fine place to sunbathe (see p117).

8 Marshall's Beach
MAP C1

Also known as Land's End Beach, diminutive Marshall's Beach is secluded almost beneath the Golden Gate Bridge, with stunning sea views and good sightings of seabirds. A clothing optional beach, Marshall's is frequented by gay residents and freethinkers. Access is via the steep Batteries to Bluffs Trail, or from popular North Baker Beach, also a nude beach. Swimming is prohibited due to strong currents.

9 Aquatic Park
MAP F1

Shielded by a horseshoe-shaped fishing pier, this is a man-made lagoon near Fisherman's Wharf, with a calm cove, a sandy beach, a stepped seawall for lounging, restrooms, and a paved walkway making it accessible to wheelchairs and bikes. This is the number-one spot from which to watch the Fourth of July fireworks and Fleet Week aerial shows.

10 East Beach
MAP D1

On the paved Bay Trail between the yacht harbor in the Marina District and Crissy Field, with dazzling Golden Gate Bridge and Alcatraz views, this is one of the only beaches where swimming is safe from undertows and currents. On site are picnic tables and grills, restrooms, lawns for lounging, and free parking.

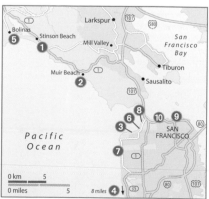

🔟 Outdoor Activities

A hiking trail on Mount Tamalpais

1 Hiking

The Bay Area is replete with magnificent hiking trails for every type of nature-lover. Land's End offers some wild terrain to scramble over *(see p119)*, and Mount Tamalpais is crisscrossed with trails *(see p126)*, but just scaling the city's hills is enough hiking for most people.

2 Swimming

MAP H2 ■ Embarcadero YMCA: 169 Steuart St ■ (415) 957-9622 ■ www.ymcasf.org

Some hotels and the Embarcadero YMCA have pools, and close-to-shore swimming can be enjoyed at a few spots, namely China Beach, the protected cove at Aquatic Park, and the shallow waters off Crissy Field – kids wade in the tidal marsh here, too.

3 Sailing

www.ocscsailing.com

Charter a yacht or a masted schooner, take sailing lessons, or tour the Bay on a motor cruiser, catamaran, or sailboat. Fun to watch are the frequent regattas and boating events, from Opening Day on the Bay to Fleet Week and the Fourth of July.

4 Skating

It's great fun to watch inline and roller skaters show-off their skills. They also offer lessons from noon to 5pm on Sundays at 5th Avenue and Kennedy Drive in Golden Gate Park. Skating can also be enjoyed on the paved path at Marina Green.

5 Running

Bay to Breakers: 3rd Sun in May ■ (415) 231-3130 ■ www.zappos baytobreakers.com; San Francisco Marathon: Jun or Jul ■ (888) 958-6668 ■ www.thesfmarathon.com

Since the restoration of Crissy Field, the Golden Gate Promenade *(see p98)* has been an inspiring run – and, of course, Golden Gate Park offers endless opportunities for jogging. If organized running is your thing, try the Bay to Breakers or the San Francisco Marathon.

6 Tennis

San Francisco Recreation and Park Department: (415) 831-2700 ■ Golden Gate Park: (415) 753-7001

Contact the Recreation and Park Department for your nearest free public tennis court. Golden Gate Park courts charge a small fee; book in advance. Most public outdoor courts are open from sunrise to sunset. Indoor courts are the purview of private tennis clubs, with membership required.

Sailing in the Bay

7 Golf

Golden Gate Park: (415) 751-8987 ■ **Lincoln Park:** (415) 221-9911 ■ **Presidio Golf Course:** (415) 561-4661 ■ **TPC Harding Park:** (415) 664-4690

TPC Harding Park has been modernized for professional tournaments, and Presidio Golf Course is among the best in the country. Locals love Lincoln Park, an affordable course above Land's End; the par 3 Golden Gate Park Golf Course; and the nine-hole Gleneagles Golf Course.

Biking near the Golden Gate Bridge

8 Biking

City Cycle: 3001 Steiner St ■ (415) 346-2242 ■ www.citycycle.com

Bicycling is big in San Francisco. Don't miss biking across the Golden Gate Bridge. Rent bikes from City Cycle.

9 Kayaking

San Francisco Kayak & Adventures: Pier 52 ■ (415) 787-2628 ■ www.sfkayak.com

Unpredictable waters and winds in the Bay call for a professional guide. While sunset paddle tours are available at Richardson Bay and Angel Island, you can enjoy a calmer experience at McCovey Cove.

10 Windsurfing

The Bay is one of the most popular windsurfing and kiteboarding sites in the world. Spectators often watch from the shoreline, especially at Crissie Field. Boardsports shops offer lessons and rentals.

TOP 10 SPECTATOR SPORTS

Levi's Stadium, home of the 49ers

1 San Francisco 49ers
4900 Marie P. DeBartolo Way, Santa Clara ■ (415) 656-4900
NFL team, plays September to January.

2 San Francisco Giants
AT&T Park, 24 Willie Mays Plaza ■ (415) 972-2000
Baseball team, plays April to October.

3 Golden State Warriors
Oracle Arena, 7000 Coliseum Way, Oakland ■ (510) 986-2222
An NBA basketball team.

4 Oakland Athletics
(510) 638-4900
Historic winners of Major League Baseball in the 1970s.

5 Oakland Raiders
(800) 724-3377
American Football League team.

6 Golden Gate Fields
1100 Eastshore Highway, Berkeley ■ (510) 559-7300
The East Bay venue for horse-racing.

7 Mazda Raceway Laguna Seca
1021 Monterey–Salinas Hwy, Salinas ■ (831) 242-8201
Grand Prix and motorcycle racing at this 2.2-mile (3.6-km) track.

8 Sonoma Raceway
29355 Arnold Dr, Sonoma ■ (707) 938-8448
Superbike and auto-racing in the Sonoma Valley.

9 San Jose Sharks
SAP Center, 525 West Santa Clara St, San Jose ■ (800) 366-4423
Fast-paced NHL ice hockey.

10 Sacramento Kings
Golden 1 Center Arena, 547 L Street, Sacramento ■ (916) 928-0000
Men's NBA basketball team.

🔟 Off the Beaten Path

The Lyon Street steps, leading into the Presidio

1 Lyon Street Steps

MAP E2 ▪ Lyon St at Broadway

Take your time climbing the Lyon Street steps adjacent to the Presidio (there are over 200) for sweeping, bird's-eye views of the Bay, the Presidio, the Palace of Fine Arts, and the manicured gardens and balconied perfection of the Pacific Heights mansions. At the top there is a gate into the Presidio.

2 Tin How Temple

MAP N4 ▪ 125 Waverly Place ▪ Open 10am–4pm daily

On a Chinatown backstreet in a colorful 19th-century building, a narrow stairway leads past a mahjongg parlor to the Tin How Temple, where incense wafts through a lantern-lit chamber dedicated to the Queen of Heaven. Be respectful, and burn a joss stick for your fortune.

3 Angel Island State Park

Belvedere Tiburon ▪ www.angelislandsf.com ▪ Café: open 10am–3pm Mon–Fri, 10am–4pm Sat & Sun

Live music and draft beer make the deck at Angel Island Café a good place to hang out on week-ends. Catch the ferry from Tiburon (see website for details) and head for the picnic tables on the lawns around Ayala Cove where sailboats, kayaks, and power yachts come and go. Walking and biking trails connect historic sites and a secluded beach.

4 Cliff's Variety

MAP E5 ▪ 479 Castro St ▪ (415) 431-5365 ▪ Open 10am–8pm Mon–Sat, 10am–6pm Sun ▪ www.cliffsvariety.com

Since 1936, this store in the heart of the Castro has been an emporium of hardware, quirky decor and kitchen utensils, toys, old-fashioned candy, and surprises. Local gay residents come for costumes, wigs, tiaras, and boas; tourists come for souvenirs and people-watching.

The SS *Jeremiah O'Brien* Liberty Ship

5 SS Jeremiah O'Brien

MAP F1 ▪ Pier 45 ▪ (415) 964-4421 ▪ Open 9am–4pm daily ▪ Adm ▪ www.ssjeremiahobrien.org

Ferrying troops and supplies during World War II, 441-ft- (134-m-) long SS *Jeremiah O'Brien* was part of the invasion of Normandy, and is one of only two restored survivors of the original 2,710 Liberty Ships. She fires up her engines on "Steaming Weekends" and there are daily tours.

6 Letterman Digital Arts Center

MAP D2 ▪ **Letterman Drive** ▪ (415) 746-5444 ▪ Open 9am–5pm Mon–Fri ▪ www.lucasfilm.com

On the east end of the Presidio, at the headquarters of Lucasfilm, Yoda tops a fountain and in the lobby you can see the Darth Vader costume and other *Star Wars* artifacts. Rest from the excitement in the lovely landscaped public park, which has views toward the Golden Gate Bridge.

7 Gospel Music at Glide Memorial Church

Crowds gather every Sunday at 9am and 11am for the joyful noise of services at Glide Memorial United Methodist Church. With a 125-voice gospel choir singing jazz, blues, and rock and roll, plus an audience made up of all ages, races, and religions, the emotional scene is set for the flamboyant Reverend Cecil Williams, who welcomes all comers *(see p48)*.

8 Yachting and Lawn Bowling in the Park

MAP B4 ▪ **Golden Gate Park** ▪ (415) 386-1037 ▪ Open 1–4pm daily & for special events ▪ www.sfmyc.org ▪ www.sflbc.org

For more than a century, the members of the Lawn Bowling Club, clad all in white, have welcomed

spectators at their greensward. The steam-powered and electric sailing vessels of the Model Yacht Club can be seen zooming across Spreckels Lake daily, particularly during the Wooden Boats on Parade event held every second year in October.

Lawn Bowling Club, Golden Gate Park

9 Cottage Row

MAP F3 ▪ **Between Sutter & Bush** ▪ (415) 391-2000 ▪ Open sunrise–sunset

The hidden gem of Cottage Row Historic District is lined with late 1800s Italianate houses from the days of horse-drawn streetcars. Around the corner are the "Painted Ladies" – elaborate Victorian houses.

10 Presidio Sculptures

MAP D2 ▪ www.presidio.gov

Sculptures by Andy Goldsworthy are set in the Presidio forest. His 100-ft- (30-m-) high *Spire*, made of cypress trees, towers in a copse. *Wood Line* is in century-old eucalyptus groves.

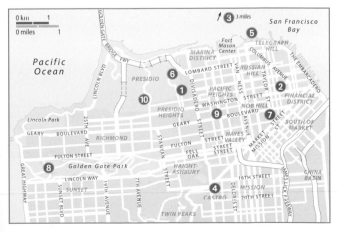

Day Trips from the City

Giant redwoods in Muir Woods

1 Muir Woods
Muir Woods National Monument ■ (415) 388-2595 ■ Open 8am–sunset daily ■ Adm ■ www.nps.gov/muwo

Named after the 19th-century conservationist, John Muir (see p47), this 1-sq mile (2-sq km) woodland is home to some of the last-remaining first-growth redwood. Some of these giants are over 1,000 years old. As parking is limited and fills up most days, reservations are required for vehicles and the Muir Woods Shuttle (see GoMuirWoods.com).

2 Big Basin Redwoods State Park
Highway 9 is one of the most picturesque drives in the Bay Area, winding its way among green mountains and through little towns on the way to this park, which, although it's a relatively short drive from Silicon Valley, has a backwoods feel.

3 Los Gatos and Saratoga
Hakone Gardens: 21000 Big Basin Way, Saratoga ■ (408) 741-4994 ■ Open 10am–5pm Mon–Fri, 11am–5pm Sat–Sun ■ Adm ■ www.hakone.com

In the hills above Silicon Valley, and below the Santa Cruz Mountains, these historic small towns offer charming shops, restaurants, and inns (see p129). One of the best things to do is to visit Hakone Gardens, a beautiful Japanese park with a tea house.

4 Monterey Peninsula
Day-trippers head to Monterey for its world-class aquarium, to shop and eat on Cannery Row (made famous by John Steinbeck), and to ramble along the shores of Point Lobos State Natural Reserve. Carmel-by-the-Sea is full of quaint cottages, art galleries, and boutique shops, as well as having a picturesque beach. Golfers make pilgrimages to visit the legendary Pebble Beach and Spanish Bay golf clubs, and to play at Bayonet Black Horse and Pacific Grove courses.

A lake in Big Basin Redwoods State Park

5 The Wine Country

Taking at least a day to drive up into the Napa and Sonoma valleys should be on everyone's San Francisco to-do list. Not only is the countryside beautiful, but also you can sample some of the best wines in the world. Dip into the restorative volcanic hot springs, and enjoy lavish spa treatments *(see pp36–9)*.

6 Stanford University

Located just 30 minutes south of the city, with a Caltrain station right at the main gates, the palm-lined beauty of this campus makes it worth a trip *(see p126)*. The visual motif of sandstone and red-tile roofs has been carried forward since the Romanesque Quadrangle was built in the late 1800s. The ornate carvings that decorate the arches and pillars are extra-ordinarily lovely, setting off the elaborate mosaic that graces the facade of the Memorial Church.

7 Half Moon Bay

This charming Victorian-era town is fringed with long, sandy beaches that are perfect for strolling and surfing. Half Moon Bay State Beach is actually made up of 3 miles (5 km) of adjacent beaches, along-side which the Coastside Trail runs. The local flower farms and busy fishing port are photogenic, while fresh seafood, art galleries, and country stores add to the mix.

8 Santa Cruz

This beach resort has always had a reputation for the vibrancy of its countercultural way of life. Along the beautiful coastline, the most prominent feature is the boardwalk's Giant Dipper Roller Coaster, which has been thrilling Santa Cruzers since 1924. The best swimming in the Bay Area is also here *(see p129)*.

9 Point Reyes

Some 110 sq miles (285 sq km) of pristine natural coastline make this promontory a haven for all sorts of wildlife and a thing of unforgettable, windswept beauty. You can watch whales and sea lions from Point Reyes Lighthouse *(see p129)*.

Point Reyes Lighthouse

10 Sonoma Coast

The Tides Wharf: 835 Coast Highway One ◾ (707) 875-3652

About an hour's scenic drive from the city are sandy beaches, rocky coves, and the fisherman's village of Bodega Bay. From the deck or a window table at the Tides Wharf seafood restaurant, watch harbor seals play and fishermen unload their catches, then take a drive along world-famous Highway 1, stopping off at Sonoma Coast beaches.

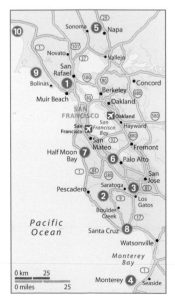

🔟 Children's Attractions

Children's Creativity Museum, Yerba Buena Gardens

1 Children's Creativity Museum

This elaborate complex, aimed both at entertaining kids and spurring their creativity to the max, is part of the greater Yerba Buena Gardens. There's an old-fashioned carousel; a labyrinth; a studio where they can script, produce, and star in their own videos; art studios; and a digital workshop, plus lots more to keep them busy all day long. Suitable for those aged 2 to 12 *(see p34)*.

2 San Francisco Zoo

Kids will never forget their direct encounters with farm animals at the zoo and visits with animal babies, which may include gorillas, snow leopards, rhinos, or alpacas. Top-quality children's programs, many feeding times and the creepy-crawly insect denizens, make it a must for budding zoologists. Extensive landscaping for wandering, and a carousel, add to the fun *(see p119)*.

3 Aquariums

Part of Golden Gate Park's California Academy of Sciences *(see pp26–7)*, the Steinhart Aquarium is a big hit with kids. The darkened corridors are filled with softly glowing tanks in which some of the weirdest creatures on the planet present themselves. Then there's the Touching Tidal Pool if kids want to get up close and personal with their finny friends. At Fisherman's Wharf, Aquarium of the Bay gives an even greater undersea experience, with walk-through transparent tunnels surrounded by sea life *(see p16)*.

4 Randall Museum

MAP E4 ■ 199 Museum Way, off Roosevelt Way, Buena Vista ■ (415) 554-9600 ■ Open 10am–5pm Tue–Sat ■ Closed Mon and public hols. ■ www.randallmuseum.org

Perched above the city, in Corona Heights Park, this small, welcoming complex has plenty of animals in the petting zoo, honeybees, a magnificent model train, a Natural Sciences Lab, ceramic studio, and a high-tech STEM lab. There are also interactive desert, riparian and urban habitats, as well as marine environments.

5 Alcatraz

"The Rock" is always a hit with older children, particularly those who enjoy the grim, quasi-military aspects of the place. The wildness of the island's natural beauty, as well as the ferry ride out and back, will also delight. Smaller kids may find it a bit frightening *(see pp18–21)*.

6 Bay Area Discovery Museum

557 McReynolds Rd, Sausalito ▪ (415) 339-3900 ▪ Open 9am–4pm Tue–Fri, 10am–5pm Sat, 9am–5pm Sun ▪ Closed public hols & last two weeks in Sep ▪ Adm ▪ www. baykidsmuseum.org

This hands-on museum on the Marin waterfront is aimed at children aged 6 months to 10 years. Kids enjoy an art studio, a science lab, a wave workshop where they learn about sea and plant life, and a media center. There are year-round day camps as well. The café offers healthy choices.

7 Exploratorium

Kids can experience one of the finest San Francisco interactive days at this superb science museum at Pier 15. They'll learn all about their senses and how they work, as well as delve into all the laws of physics through first-hand experiments, like making simple circuit boards. The top draw, however, is the Tactile Dome, a dark sphere in which you feel your way along, touching a range of sensorially stimulating objects and textures (see p88).

Making circuit boards, Exploratorium

8 Golden Gate Park Playground

At the southeastern corner of the park, kids will love the old carousel, a treehouse, and some great swings, slides, and other kid-orientated rides. There is also a towering rope climbing structure and a climbing wall shaped like waves (see pp24–5).

Angel Island State Park

9 Angel Island State Park

Angel Island is an ideal place for a full-day family outing. You can picnic, swim, hike, kayak, camp, or take the tram tour that goes all around the island, with a guide who points out sites of historic interest – dating from the days when the place was a rather forbidding immigrant clearing station (see p96).

10 Metreon

Intended as a bustling, high-tech, multilevel amusement arcade for adolescents, this enormous shopping centre has an extremely impressive IMAX 3D movie theatre. Here you can watch the latest Hollywood blockbusters and chart-toppers with full digital sound effects amped up to the highest possible level. Otherwise, the Metreon offers several different restaurant choices and great views over the city from the fourth-floor deck space (see p34).

Performing Arts Venues

War Memorial Opera House and San Francisco Ballet

1 War Memorial Opera House and San Francisco Ballet

MAP R1 ▪ 301 Van Ness Ave ▪ (415) 864-3330 ▪ www.sfwmpac.org

The San Francisco Opera Company is one of the largest in the country and performs here from May to December. The excellent San Francisco Ballet, one of the nation's oldest ballet companies, mostly performs at the War Memorial Opera House.

2 Louise M. Davies Symphony Hall

MAP R1 ▪ 201 Van Ness Ave ▪ (415) 864-6000 ▪ www.sfsymphony.org

With performances from September through to May, under the directorship of Michael Tilson Thomas, the San Francisco Symphony Orchestra performs in this glass-fronted modern structure with its carefully modulated acoustics. Look out for the Henry Moore bronze sculpture out front. World-famous orchestras, conductors and artists – from China to Israel, and Japan to the UK – can be found on the program, along with holiday productions.

3 Masonic Auditorium

MAP N3 ▪ 1111 California St ▪ (415) 776-7457 ▪ www.sfmasonic.com

Originally a Masonic Temple, built in 1957, this attractive structure, with its 3,300-seat auditorium, is used as a venue for lectures, and readings, jazz performances, as well as conventions and seminars. The mosaics depict some of the tenets of Freemasonry.

4 Curran Theater

MAP P3 ▪ 445 Geary St ▪ (888) 746 1799 ▪ www.shnsf.com

After the renovation of its grand 1922 structure in 2017, the Curran now houses a range of productions, from the *Bright Star* bluegrass musical by Steve Martin, to edgy *Fun Home*, a musical about the coming of age in a queer world. Three glamorous new bars add to the ambiance.

5 Beach Blanket Babylon

MAP L4 ▪ Club Fugazi, 678 Beach Blanket Babylon Blvd ▪ (415) 421-4222 ▪ www. beachblanketbabylon.com

High camp and high headdresses, with jolly singing by the veteran ensemble cast, make this one of the joys of the city. It's been zinging the heartstrings of lovers of San Francisco for

Singer, Beach Blanket Babylon

more than a quarter of a century and shows no signs of flagging. The excuse for all this frivolity is the sending up of various notables, most of whom well deserve the good-natured ribbing.

6 Orpheum Theatre
MAP R2 ■ 1192 Market St ■ (888) 746-1799 ■ www.shnsf.com

Originally a vaudeville house and then a movie theater, this is the historic spot where *Hair* was given its first West Coast performance some 30 years ago – known locally as "the New York version of what happened here in San Francisco." Concerts and theater performances range from Billy Joel and Bruno Mars to *The Lion King* and *Les Misérables*.

Orpheum Theatre

7 SFJAZZ Center
MAP R1 ■ 201 Franklin St at Fell St ■ (866) 920-5299 ■ www.sfjazz.org

With specially designed acoustics and an intimate concert hall, the luminous building that houses the SFJAZZ Center is the first in the US to be specifically built for jazz performances. The center aims to educate and inspire audiences with an eclectic program of events from world-class musicians.

8 Golden Gate Theatre
MAP Q3 ■ 1 Taylor St ■ (888) 746-1799 ■ www.shnsf.com

This former movie house, designed with Moorish influences in the 1920s, is one of the city's larger mainstream theaters. Its usual offerings are traveling Broadway blockbusters, such as *Aladdin*, *The Book of Mormon*, and *Waitress*.

9 American Conservatory Theater (ACT)
MAP P3 ■ Geary Theater, 405 Geary St ■ (415) 749-2228 ■ www.act-sf.org

Founded in the 1960s, San Francisco's most important theater company is internationally respected and has produced premieres of a number of major plays. At the heart of ACT is one of the most acclaimed actor-training institutions in the nation – former students include Annette Bening and Denzel Washington.

10 Magic Theatre
MAP F1 ■ Fort Mason Center, Bldg D ■ (415) 441-8822 ■ www.magictheatre.org

In the 1970s, none other than Sam Shepard was the resident playwright of the Magic, and its stage has seen performances by the likes of Sean Penn and Nick Nolte. It specializes in new plays, usually by up-and-coming Americans, and also offers "raw play" readings of as yet unstaged works.

Nightlife

The Tonga Room and Hurricane Bar offer a South Sea Island theme

1 The Tonga Room and Hurricane Bar

MAP N3 ▪ Fairmont Hotel, 950 Mason St ▪ (415) 772 5278 ▪ www.tongaroom.com

This Nob Hill tiki bar is almost Disneyesque in its tropical effects, including indoor monsoons and a floating band. Aimed at grown-ups of every age, it has delivered kitschy Polynesian dazzlement since 1945, and is often chosen as the venue for birthday celebrations. The bar's award-winning weekday happy hour (5–7pm) includes an Asian buffet at nominal cost.

2 Great Northern

One of the few San Francisco venues large enough to be considered a proper dance club, Great Northern is well known for hip-hop shows and international house DJs. It is beloved by club-goers for its great variety of music, its size, and its revolving art collection *(see p113)*.

3 Mezzanine

Located in the SoMa district, industrial-chic Mezzanine comprises one large room with a long bar and a concrete dance floor. Mezzanine hosts live music from touring indie bands, esoteric hip-hop acts, and visiting DJs *(see p114)*.

4 Bottom of the Hill

Open seven days a week in Potrero Hill, this is one of the best live-music venues in a city renowned for its live music. Even though Bottom of the Hill has a definite punk vibe, you are just as likely to hear a folk music act playing as a hard-core punk band. If you don't care for the music, just head to the back where you can grab a table out of earshot *(see p114)*.

5 Starlight Room

MAP P4 ▪ Sir Francis Drake Hotel, 450 Powell St at Sutter ▪ (415) 395-8595 ▪ www.starlightroomsf.com

Something for those who enjoy dancing, good views, and great cocktails. Twenty-one stories above Union Square, couples can dance to jazz and the milder R&B hits, and

Starlight Room

relax in the easy sophistication of this place. The theme is 1930s-stylish, so consider it a chance to dress up in smart suits and party dresses, sip highballs, and enjoy the city's seductive lights. "Sunday's A Drag" brunch features the city's best performances by drag queens.

The Great American Music Hall

6 Bimbo's 365 Club
MAP K3 ■ 1025 Columbus Ave ■ (415) 474-0365 ■ www.bimbos365 club.com

Whether you are into swing, jazz, or rock, this San Francisco institution delivers. A retro-chic yet unpretentious music venue since 1931, this hopping bar with glittering decor and an old-school feel brings in all the top acts. Their old-fashioned New Year's Eve parties are legendary.

7 The Hidden Vine
MAP M5 ■ 408 Merchant St ■ (415) 674-3567 ■ www.thehidden vine.com

Classy, cozy wine bar with a selection of close to 180 types of wine from all over the world. The diverse food menu contains specialties such as cheese charcuterie platters, as well as organic, seasonal tapas. A different wine region is featured every month. The Vine is ranked as one of the top ten wine bars in America by *USA Today*. With a large group, reserve the *bocce* court.

8 Cityscape Lounge 44
MAP G3 ■ Hilton San Francisco Union Square at 333 O'Farrell St ■ (415) 923-5002 ■ www.cityscapesf.com

Housed on the 46th floor of the Hilton, this is a perfect spot for romantic nights. It offers sparkling 360-degree views of the city skyline. Take the Tower 1 elevator for signature cocktails, top Californian wines, and delicious dishes from the small plate menu.

9 Great American Music Hall
MAP P1 ■ 859 O'Farrell St ■ (415) 885-0750 ■ www.slimspresents.com

With a colorful history, the Great American Music Hall is the place to see live music, from indie, rock and country, to folk, jazz, and blues. The views from the Victorian balcony are great and the sound quality is top-notch. Downstairs has standing room only. Food and drinks are available.

10 Punch Line Comedy Club
MAP M5 ■ 444 Battery St ■ (415) 397-7573 ■ www.punchline comedyclub.com

An alternative to bar-hopping, there is no better venue for a good laugh than this hilarious comedy club. National, as well as local acts, headline a fun evening in an intimate setting, with all the seating up close to the stage. Buy tickets in advance to ensure seats.

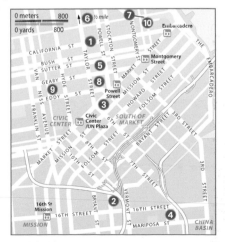

TOP10 Gay and Lesbian Venues

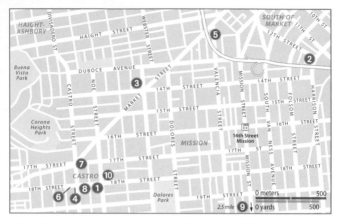

1 Moby Dick
MAP E5 ▪ 4049 18th St
▪ (415) 861-1199

This old-time Castro hangout attracts a more mature crowd. It's generally a bunch of regulars getting together for pinball or pool. The windows are big, so you can keep track of what's going down on the street. The music is largely 1980s retro, which sets a fun-loving tone.

2 SF Eagle
MAP G4 ▪ 398 12th St

Bikers and leather boys still rule at this venerable SoMa dive. Come here to revel in the beer-busting, testosterone-filled atmosphere. The back patio gets going on Sunday afternoons, and Thursdays feature performances by local bands.

3 Churchill in the Castro
MAP F4 ▪ 198 Church St
▪ (415) 570-9198

Located in the Castro district, this cocktail bar is set in military barracks inspired by those used in World War II. It features vintage artifacts, as well as pool tables, and serves top-notch cocktails in mason jars. It also offers fine wines and a variety of draft and bottled beers.

4 Harvey's
MAP E5 ▪ 500 Castro St at 18th ▪ (415) 431-4278

Named in honor of the slain gay politician Harvey Milk *(see p47)*, this is the ideal place to get to know the look and feel of the

Harvey's in Castro Disctrict

Castro district. There's lots of gay memorabilia on the walls, the staff are friendly, the ambience easygoing, and not at all quirky or kinky. It's the more wholesome face of gay San Francisco. Happy hour lasts from 3 to 6pm on weekdays only.

5 Martuni's
MAP F4 ■ 4 Valencia St at Market ■ (415) 241-0205

With its decor of glass and chrome and the regulars' penchant for singing old torch songs, this is a very retro piano bar for an older gay crowd. It's a magnet for butch guys, drag queens, and straights, too – anyone who likes a good singalong – or who doesn't mind embarrassing themselves on the microphone.

6 Badlands
MAP E5 ■ 4121 18th St ■ (415) 626-9320

Its old, dingy interior used to live up to its menacing name, but no more since it has gone all slick and shiny. Still, it's a big draw for the under-40 set. The Sunday afternoon beer bust (2–8pm) is, for many, the most happening event of the week.

Neon sign outside Twin Peaks

7 Twin Peaks
MAP E5 ■ 401 Castro St ■ (415) 864-9470

Conveniently located on the corner of Market Street, this legendary and distinctive tavern offers one of the best views of the Castro, whether by day or night. The interior is an inviting, pillowed triangular space with plate-glass windows.

Interior of Midnight Sun

8 Midnight Sun
MAP E5 ■ 4067 18th St ■ (415) 861-4186

This popular, posy video bar fills up quickly after office hours and stays that way until the wee hours. Mostly frequented by good-looking 20- and 30-somethings, it's more about being admired than making connections here, so it's best to go with a friend or two, have a drink, and then move on to some livelier venue. The video screens show a mix of music clips and TV sitcoms. Drinks are two for one until 9pm every day of the week.

9 Sundance Saloon
MAP G6 ■ 550 Barneveld Ave near Hwys 280 and 101 ■ (415) 820-1403 ■ www.sundancesaloon.org

Wear your Stetson and boots at this large country-and-western dance club. Two-step and line-dance lessons are offered twice weekly for all ages. The saloon also hosts various special events.

10 Last Call Bar
MAP E5 ■ 3988 18th St ■ (415) 861 1310 ■ www.thelast callbar.com

Friendly, unpretentious dive bar with an Irish pub-like atmosphere, complete with a jukebox machine, two large screens that cater to sports fans, and a cozy fireplace to keep warm on cold and foggy days. Happy hour begins at noon and lasts till 7pm every day.

 Restaurants

Intimate and modern interior at two-Michelin-starred Quince

1 Quince
Run by Michelin-starred chef Michael Tusk, Quince is considered by many to be the best restaurant in the city. It serves dish after dish of beautiful Californian fare, influenced by northern Italy and made with the freshest local ingredients (see p95).

2 Gitane
Worth a visit as much for its dramatic, gypsy bordello atmosphere as for its delicious Iberian entrées. Drawing on the rich cuisines of Portugal, Morocco, southern Spain, and France, Gitane offers mouth-watering tagines as well as lamb, pork, and fish dishes, all of which are served with considerable flair and lots of flavor (see p95).

3 La Mar
Surprisingly, La Mar is one of San Francisco's few top-notch seafood restaurants. It serves wonderful, super-fresh Peruvian seafood (including an astounding assortment of tasty ceviches) in a stunning blue and white dining room looking out over the Bay (see p95).

4 A16
Known for its authentic Neapolitan pizzas, fresh pastas, house-cured salami, and regional wines, this casual yet chic marina restaurant will transport you straight to southern Italy (see p101).

5 Greens
The first fine-dining vegetarian restaurant in the city (see p101), Annie Sommerville's famous eatery was inspired by the huge success of the former Zen bakery and coffee shop. The drinks menu only features organic and sustainable wines. This spacious, pleasant Marina restaurant came to define vegetarian cuisine for the Bay Area.

6 Nopalito
From the folks at Nopa comes a fresh take on Mexican fare. Nopalito focuses on traditional Mexican street food – including carnitas and taquitos (see p107). The cocktails are just as fantastic as the food itself, but be prepared to wait.

7 Foreign Cinema
In the courtyard, a selection of old and new movies are projected onto a neighboring building while you dine. The Mediterranean-influenced food is also excellent and the oyster bar and Sunday brunch are popular (see p115).

8 Lers Ros Thai

Lers Ros delivers authentic Thai dishes in a no-frills, casual dining room. Arrive early or you'll be standing in line down the street. Reservations are also available *(see p95)*.

9 Delfina

Thanks to its perfect, modern Italian fare made with the freshest local ingredients, it has been hard to get a table at Delfina for years now, which is saying a lot in a city that has trendy restaurants opening every month. In addition to the legendary chicken and delicate pasta dishes at Delfina, you can indulge in the best Neapolitan pizza outside of Italy at its pizzeria next door *(see p115)*.

10 Spruce

This once Michelin-starred restaurant's excellent seasonal Nouveau American menu has a major meat focus. For the same delicious food with a slightly less formal feel, opt to sit in the bar *(see p107)*.

Pastrami sandwich, Spruce

TOP 10 ROMANTIC DINNER SPOTS

Cliff House

1 Cliff House
A wild setting with views of crashing waves *(see p123)*.

2 Atelier Crenn
MAP E2 = 3127 Fillmore = (415) 440-0460 = $$$
Delicious food, and the dining room is intimate and quiet.

3 Acquerello
MAP N1 = 1722 Sacramento St = (415) 567-5432 = $$$
The black truffles are an aphrodisiac.

4 Forbes Island
MAP J4 = Pier 39 = (415) 951-4900 = $$$
Located beneath a lighthouse.

5 Boulevard
MAP H2 = 1 Mission St = (415) 543-6084 = $$$
Belle époque decor and superb food.

6 BIX
Stylish spot with retro decor and atmospheric live music *(see p94)*.

7 Mourad
MAP G3 = 140 New Montgomery St = (415) 660-2500 = $$$
Dine on Moroccan food, whilst sat in a booth, in a historic building.

8 Gary Danko
MAP K2 = 800 N Point St = (415) 749-2060 = $$$
Sophisticated contemporary cuisine.

9 Frascati
MAP L2 = 1901 Hyde St = (415) 928-1406 = $$
Italian fare and great views.

10 Chez Panisse
1517 Shattuck Ave, Berkeley, off Hwy 80 = (510) 548-5525 = $$$
The birthplace of Cal-Med cuisine. Book weeks ahead.

For a key to restaurant price ranges see p95

🔟 Cafés and Bars

1 The Buena Vista Café

Opened in 1916 at the cable car turnaround at Fisherman's Wharf, this friendly bar and eatery claims to have been the first to introduce Irish coffee to America in 1952. First served at Shannon Airport in Ireland, the drink is composed of Irish whiskey, a sugar cube, hot coffee, and a foamy collar of whipped cream *(see p101)*.

2 Caffè Trieste

A North Beach landmark that must be experienced if you have any interest whatsoever in the colorful history of this quarter – whether it is from the literary and artistic point of view, or for the Italian culture. It's a great place for a cup of whatever warm liquid you favor, and to sit and people-watch, or dip into one of San Francisco's free weekly newspapers *(see p94)*.

3 Blue Bottle Café

This hip coffee roaster kicked off San Francisco's latest café trend; it serves up perfect cappuccinos and lattes in its chic, industrial SoMa space. Also on offer are Kyoto-style iced coffees, brewed using the Japanese slow-drip method. Perfection takes time, however, and these baristas take their work very seriously, so be prepared for a bit of a wait. The experience is worth trying at least once *(see p94)*.

Slow-drip brewers, Blue Bottle Café

Fresh bread, Tartine Bakery and Café

4 Tartine Bakery and Café
MAP F5 ▪ 600 Guerrero St ▪ (415) 487-2600

You may find a line out the door at this purveyor of rustic breads, "hot pressed" sandwiches, pizzas, cakes, and tarts. The co-owners have both been awarded the James Beard Award for Outstanding Pastry Chefs.

5 Réveille Coffee Co.
MAP E5 ▪ 4076 18th St ▪ (415) 789-6258

Coffee aficionados gather at this neighborhood café in the Castro (there are also branches in North Beach and Jackson Square) for meticulously-crafted espresso. Watch the buzzing street from the patio as you enjoy homemade granola, sandwiches, or flatbreads.

6 Tosca Café
MAP M4 ▪ 242 Columbus Ave ▪ (415) 986-9651

Owned by English celebrity chef April Bloomfield, Tosca offers Italian deli-cacies to enjoy while sipping cocktails and listening to opera on the jukebox.

7 Dolores Park Café
▪ MAP F5 ▪ 501 Dolores St ▪ (415) 621-2936

This funky neighborhood café has it all – views of Dolores Park, filling breakfast and lunch fare, home-made smoothies, freshly baked pastries, and live music and spoken word performances on Friday nights.

8 Bourbon & Branch

You'll need the nightly password to enter this bar. Once inside, enjoy inventive cocktails in one of the most beautifully designed bars in the city, and explore the many secret rooms *(see p114)*.

9 Vesuvio Café

MAP M4 ■ 255 Columbus Ave ■ (415) 362-3370

Since 1948, Vesuvio has been the North Beach haunt of artists, writers, and bon vivants of all stripes, many of whom wander across the street to the famous City Lights Bookstore *(see p92)* and back.

10 Smuggler's Cove

MAP F3 ■ 650 Gough St ■ (415) 869-1900

The quirky pirate-ship decor creates a fun setting for this three-level tiki bar with a menu of rums, Caribbean cocktails, and classic libations from Prohibition-era Havana.

Selection of rum at Smuggler's Cove

TOP 10 BRUNCH VENUES

French toast

1 Dottie's True Blue Café
MAP G3 ■ 28 6th St ■ Closed Tue, Wed
It's a SoMa tradition to stand in line for the American breakfasts served here.

2 Sears Fine Food
A Union Square institution, noted for its silver dollar pancakes *(see p95)*.

3 Ella's
MAP E3 ■ 500 Presidio Ave
Expect to wait at this breakfast haven, which has been operating for 20 years.

4 Mama's on Washington Square
MAP L4 ■ 1701 Stockton St ■ Closed Mon
The greatest French toast in town.

5 The Butler & The Chef Bistro
MAP G3 ■ 155A S Park St
French bistro serving the best croque monsieurs and eggs Benedict.

6 Presidio Social Club
MAP E2 ■ 563 Ruger St
An elegant restaurant serving up old-school drinks and brunch classics.

7 Just for You Café
MAP H5 ■ 732 22nd St
Soul food-inspired brunch in the Dogpatch neighborhood.

8 Kate's Kitchen
MAP F4 ■ 471 Haight St
Huge portions of breakfast specialties, including a "French Toast Orgy."

9 Chloe's Café
MAP F6 ■ 1399 Church St at 26th
Banana or pecan pancakes, and cinnamon French toast.

10 Red Door Café
MAP F3 ■ 1608 Bush St
This café is as beloved for its comical owner as for its fluffy omelets and perfect French toast.

🔟 Stores and Shopping Centers

Ferry Building Marketplace

1 Ferry Building Marketplace
MAP H2 ■ Embarcadero at Market

Wander through one of the world's greatest gourmet food markets and stop to taste fresh oysters, Vietnamese or Mexican food, salumi, Blue Bottle coffee, pastries, chocolates, and cheesecake. Visit the outdoor Saturday farmers' market on the pier.

2 Nordstrom
MAP Q4 ■ Westfield San Francisco Centre, 865 Market St

Located on the top five floors of the Westfield Centre, the fashion emporium is known as the "store in the sky." Impeccable service, a vast selection, and a refined atmosphere featuring live piano music make this a very upscale shopping experience.

3 Neiman Marcus
MAP P4 ■ 150 Stockton St

After maxing out your credit cards with designer apparel at Neiman Marcus's concessions, grab a quick bite in the Fresh Market, or linger at The Rotunda for fine dining, or high tea, under the stained-glass dome, whilst admiring the views.

4 Gump's
MAP P4 ■ 135 Post St

Founded in 1861 by German immigrants, this homegrown department store has one of the largest collections in the US of fine china and crystal, selling famous names such as Baccarat, Lalique, and Georg Jensen silver. For more designer options continue down Post Street to Crocker Galleria.

5 Macy's
MAP P4 ■ 170 O'Farrell St

This five-story landmark in Union Square is an upscale department store selling home utilities, as well as clothing for all ages. The lower level features various food outlets from Starbucks to an upscale burger bar, a bakery, and an ice cream parlor. Be sure to admire the spectacular seasonal window displays.

6 Barney's New York
MAP G3 ■ 77 O'Farrell St

Barney's is the place to go for designer clothes, shoes, and accessories from the likes of Marc Jacobs and Comme des Garçons. It has one of the best fragrance departments in the city.

7 Saks Fifth Avenue
MAP P4 ■ 384 Post St

For decades, the name Saks has been synonymous with high style, and this branch of the New York mainstay is one of the best embodiments of the store's mythic élan. You'll find just about every international designer of note here.

Saks Fifth Avenue

⑧ Embarcadero Centre
MAP N6 ■ Embarcadero & Battery, Sacramento & Clay Sts

Four high-rise blocks connect to form this sprawling shopping center. Dominated by chain stores such as Gap, it's probably not the best place to find a unique souvenir. The upper floors host restaurants and a movie theater.

Ghirardelli Square, Fisherman's Wharf

⑨ Ghirardelli Square
MAP K1 ■ 900 North Point St

Housing about 20 restaurants and shops, this former chocolate factory has become one of the most frequented destinations in Fisherman's Wharf (see p16). The stores range from tourist T-shirt shops to fine jewelry boutiques.

⑩ Westfield San Francisco Centre
MAP Q4 ■ 865 Market St

This huge center has ten levels and nearly 400 stores, including Bloomingdale's, a movie theater, and a gourmet food area.

TOP 10 SHOPPING AREAS

Grant Avenue

1 Grant Avenue
MAP N4
Chic shopping off Union Square, exotic Chinatown emporiums, and North Beach hangouts in Upper Grant.

2 Union Street
Converted Victorian homes house a charming assortment of boutiques, bookstores, antiques shops, restaurants, and art galleries (see p103).

3 Union Square
Traditionally the focal point of all the best stores, including Tiffany & Co, Armani, Cartier, Gucci, Chanel, and more (see p89).

4 Upper Fillmore Street
MAP E2
A colorful choice of cafés, restaurants, and boutiques, all geared to a high-end Pacific Heights clientele.

5 Market Street
MAP Q3
A good place to find cut-rate electronics and outlet stores, as well as the Westfield San Francisco Centre.

6 Hayes Valley
These blocks offer galleries and stores with an avant-garde feel (see p105).

7 Chestnut Street
MAP K1
Clothing boutiques, health-food shops, and an old-fashioned cinema.

8 The Mission
Plenty of discount stores and funky home furnishing shops (see p110–11).

9 Castro Street
Fine shops, gay bookstores and erotic boutiques (see p109).

10 Haight Street
The place for secondhand clothing, emporiums, and shoe stores (see p104).

TOP10 San Francisco for Free

The Music Concourse, Golden Gate Park

1 Outdoor Summer Concerts

Sigmund Stern Recreation Grove at 19th Ave & Sloat Blvd ■ **(415) 252-6252** ■ **Jun– Aug: Sun** ■ **www.sterngrove.org**

Pines and eucalyptus create a verdant backdrop for the grassy amphitheater where the free Stern Grove Festival concerts take place on summer Sundays. Thousands picnic while enjoying jazz, rock, the symphony, ballet, and opera.

2 Waterfront Ramble
The Wave Organ: MAP E1
■ **83 Marina Green Drive**

There is a lot to enjoy for free along the waterfront. Listen to *The Wave Organ*, an acoustic wave-activated sculpture, peruse murals in the Maritime Museum *(see p53)*, stroll the Hyde Street Pier past the 1886 square-rigged ship *Balcutha*, watch sea lions at Pier 39, or bask in the misty *Fog Bridge* installation at the Exploratorium *(see p88)*.

3 Bayside View of the San Francisco Giants
MAP H3 ■ **Giants Promenade**

During baseball season, it's free to watch the San Francisco Giants play at home in the AT&T Park from the Giants Promenade walkway.

4 Golden Gate Park
Opera in the Park:
■ **www.sfopera.com**

This 1.5-sq-mile (4-sq-km) urban garden is a great place to watch tai chi classes, swing dancing, or bison roaming in their paddock *(see pp24– 5)*. The Music Concourse hosts free concerts in summer, including the annual Opera in the Park event.

5 Fort Point National Historic Site

Situated at the foot of the Golden Gate Bridge, this fortress was built in 1861 to protect the city of San Francisco from Confederate attacks that never came. Children in partic- ular love to see the cannons being loaded, as well as the Civil War reenactments *(see p47)*.

Cannon at Fort Point

6 Guided Walking Tours
(415) 557-4266
■ www.sfcityguides.org

Dozens of daily, free walking tours are led by savvy locals and historians, giving insights into Coit Tower murals, Chinatown alleys, the gay Castro, Victorian architecture, the Gold Rush, and other topics.

7 City Hall
Wander through the 1915 Beaux Arts City Hall, situated in the Civic Center (see p89), which houses city government and public art. Tour guides tell of glory days and tragedies, such as the 1906 earthquake and the assassination of Mayor George Moscone in 1978 (see p43).

8 Free Museum Days
The first Tuesday of every month, museums open their doors for free, including the de Young Museum (see pp28–9), the European-art-filled Legion of Honor (see p52), the contemporary-focused Yerba Buena Center for the Arts (see p34), and the San Francisco Museum of Craft and Design (see p53). Set in a stunning Beaux Arts edifice, the Asian Art Museum is free on the first Sunday of the month (see pp52–3).

9 The Presidio
The Officers' Club:
■ www.presidioofficersclub.com

Take a ranger-led tour to experience 200 years of military history, from Spanish cannons to Civil War barracks. The Officers' Club also runs free cultural events. Meander the forest trails and enjoy a picnic on the beach or in the seaview meadows (see pp98–9).

10 Golden Gate Bridge
Whether under cloudy or sunny skies, a walk or cycle across the "international orange" Golden Gate Bridge is a must. The iconic symbol of the city towers 260 ft (79 m) above churning Bay waters, and offers spectacular views of Alcatraz Island, sailboats, freighters, and ferries (see pp12–13).

TOP 10 MONEY-SAVING TIPS

Hardly Strictly Bluegrass festival

1 One of the largest multi-genre music festivals in the country, 3-day Hardly Strictly Bluegrass is free to all. **www.hardlystrictlybluegrass.com**

2 Go San Francisco Card holders get free and discounted admission to more than 25 attractions, tours, and cruises. **www.smartdestinations.com**

3 Print out the current SF Travel Coupons for discounted cruises, tours, attractions, shopping, and more. **www.sftravelcoupons.com**

4 Tix Bay Area sells half-price tickets to cultural events, both online and at the booth on Union Square. **www.tixbayarea.org**

5 Self-cater and picnic with locally sourced food from the city's world-famous farmers' markets. **www.cafarmersmkts.com**

6 Happy-hour bar menus of small plates and discounted drinks are available from about 4pm to 7pm.

7 Discount coupons and special offers are available on the San Francisco Travel website, or at the Visitor Information Center (900 Market St). **www.sftravel.com/deals**

8 At some Mexican places in the Mission, delicious burritos and tacos are under $5. Chinese restaurants and food trucks also offer good value.

9 Muni has 1-day and 1-month passes offering great savings. The Clipper Pass is an all-in-one prepay pass, accepted on most transport (see pp134–5).

10 The FunCheap website lists up-to-date free and inexpensive activities and events. Check the "today" and "weekend" calendars for what's free. **www.sf.funcheap.com**

Festivals and Parades

1 Chinese New Year
Jan or Feb

This is the biggest Chinese New Year celebration outside Asia. It incorporates traditional displays and the parade of dragons and performers that winds through the streets of Chinatown.

Performer, Chinese New Year parade

2 St. Patrick's Day Parade
Sat or Sun before Mar 17

With San Francisco's large Irish population, not to mention the 25 or so Irish pubs scattered around town, the St. Patrick's Day Parade and the revelry that follows into the night is one of the city's largest celebrations. The parade journeys from 2nd and Market Streets to the Civic Center.

3 Cherry Blossom Festival
Two weekends in Apr

Japantown (see p103) comes to life spectacularly when the cherry trees blossom during April. There are displays of traditional arts and crafts, *taiko* drumming, martial arts demonstrations, and dancing, as well as delicious Japanese food, making this one of the city's favorite celebrations. There is also a colorful and impressive parade.

4 Cinco de Mayo
Sat or Sun before May 5

Commemorating the defeat of the French army at Puebla, Mexico, in 1862, by General Ignacio Zaragoza, this is one of the Latino community's biggest annual festivals, featuring parades, fireworks, music, and dancing. In addition to the Civic Center, much of the fun happens in the Mission District.

5 Carnaval
Mission District ▪ Last weekend in May

Having nothing at all to do with Lent or any other traditional date, San Francisco's Carnaval is staged when the weather will most likely be at its best for the glittery event. Groups work all year long, with the help of municipal grants, to create their dazzling costumes and put together their infectiously rhythmic routines, all to a samba, rumba, or salsa beat.

6 San Francisco Pride
Sun in late Jun

More than 500,000 people attend this amazing gay event, the largest of its kind in the US, that takes over Market Street, from the Civic Center to the Embarcadero. It's up to 4 hours of Dykes on Bikes®, drag queens in nuns' habits, gay marching

San Francisco Pride

TOP 10 FAIRS AND GATHERINGS

Fillmore Jazz Festival

1 Tet Festival
Jan–Feb
A multicultural party, but mainly Vietnamese-American in theme.

2 Tribal & Textile Arts Show
Early Feb
Arts and crafts fair at the Fort Mason Center, with pottery, jewelry, and more.

3 Bay to Breakers
Late May
Runners race in funny costumes from the Ferry Building to Ocean Beach.

4 Haight-Ashbury Street Fair
Jun
You'll see hippiedom is still alive after attending this Gathering of the Tribe.

5 North Beach Festival
Jun
The city's oldest street fair features arts and crafts and some great Italian food.

6 Fillmore Jazz Festival
Early Jul
Playing up the jazz heritage of this area, with crafts and live music.

7 Ghirardelli Square Chocolate Festival
Early Sep
A chocoholic's dream, with the chance to sample various nibbles.

8 Folsom Street Fair
Last Sun Sep
One of the biggest events for the gay community after Pride.

9 Castro Street Fair
Early Oct
A build-up to Halloween, it focuses attention on everyday gay life.

10 Folsom Renaissance Faire
Mid-Oct: Sat–Sun
This delightfully rowdy event re-creates Elizabethan England.

Airshow, Fleet Week

hands, muscle men, and much more. The floats – as well as the cheering throngs – are likely to be the most over-the-top, outlandish things you've ever witnessed.

 Stern Grove Festival
Sun, early Jun–late Aug
A much-loved San Francisco tradition, this festival showcases every kind of music in an idyllic atmosphere *(see p118)*.

 Independence Day
Jul 4
This festival, held from Aquatic Park to PIER 39, involves live entertainment, food stalls, and fireworks launched from several points along the Bayfront. If it's foggy, the bursts of light seem even more romantic.

 Fleet Week
Oct
A celebration of US naval forces, air shows, and a parade of ships sail into the Bay with the spectacular San Francisco skyline as a backdrop.

10 Halloween
Oct 31
This boisterous Castro party and parade is a time for dress-up, dress-down, or undress, as the case may be; let your imagination run wild.

San Francisco Area by Area

The Downtown skyline behind the "Painted Ladies" of Alamo Square

Downtown

The Downtown area is small but highly varied, including some of the city's oldest and newest landmarks. Colorful Chinatown, exuberant North Beach, posh Nob and Russian Hills, the bustling Financial District, the graceful Ferry Building, and the architecture and culture of Civic Center; all these and more are packed into the city's heart. This is where you can ride the cable cars' most scenic routes *(see pp14–15)* and climb up Telegraph Hill, where Coit Tower stands as one of the city's most loved landmarks, competing with the Transamerica Pyramid not far away.

Chinatown statue

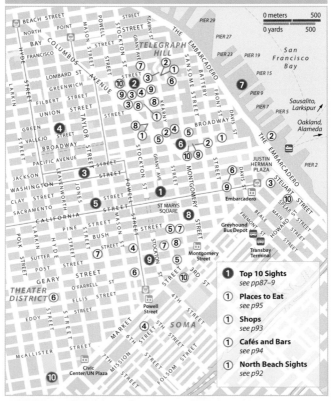

DOWNTOWN

0 meters 500
0 yards 500

San Francisco Bay

Sausalito, Larkspur

Oakland, Alameda

JUSTIN HERMAN PLAZA

Embarcadero

Greyhound Bus Depot

Transbay Terminal

Montgomery Street

ST MARYS SQUARE

THEATER DISTRICT

Powell Street

SOMA

Civic Center/UN Plaza

1 Top 10 Sights
see pp87–9

1 Places to Eat
see p95

1 Shops
see p93

1 Cafés and Bars
see p94

1 North Beach Sights
see p92

Chinatown

Since its beginnings in the 1850s, this densely populated neighborhood has held its own powerful cultural identity despite every threat and cajolery. To walk along its cluttered, clattering streets and alleys is to be transported to another continent and into another way of life – truly a "city" within the city (see pp22–3).

North Beach
MAP L4

This lively neighborhood is the original "Little Italy" of the city, and is still noted for its great Italian restaurants and cafés, mostly lined up along and near Columbus Avenue. In the 1950s, it was also a magnet for the Beat writers and poets, notably Jack Kerouac and Allen Cinsberg (see p44), who brought to the area a bohemian style which it still sports today. This is a great place for nightlife, from the tawdry bawdiness of Broadway strip joints to the simple pleasures of listening to a mezzo-soprano while you sip your cappuccino.

Nob Hill
MAP N3

With the advent of the cable car, the highest hill in San Francisco was quickly peopled with the elaborate mansions of local magnates – in particular, the "Big Four" who built the Transcontinental Railroad (see p47) – and the name has become synonymous with wealth and power. The 1906 earthquake, however, left only one "palace" standing, now the Pacific Union Club, which still proudly dominates the center of the summit. Today, instead of private mansions, Nob Hill is home to the city's fanciest hotels and apartment buildings, as well as Grace Cathedral.

Russian Hill
MAP M2

Another of San Francisco's precipitous heights, one side of which is so steep you'll find no street at all, only steps. The most famous feature of this hill is the charming Lombard Street switchback – "The World's Crookedest Street" – which attests to the hill's notoriously unmanageable inclines. As with Nob Hill, with the cable car's advent, Russian Hill was claimed by the wealthy, and it maintains a lofty position in San Francisco society to this day. It supposedly took its name from the burial place of Russian fur traders, who were among the first Europeans to ply their trade at this port in the early 1800s.

Grace Cathedral
MAP N3 ■ 1100 California St ■ (415) 749-6300 ■ Open from 8am daily (7am Thu), closing hours vary ■ www.gracecathedral.org

Inspired by French Gothic architecture, with dazzling stained-glass windows and towers topping 170 ft (50 m), this Episcopal cathedral is a photogenic landmark on Nob Hill.

Stained glass at Grace Cathedral

THE MAKING OF A CITY

The Bay lay undiscovered by Europeans until 1769, and for years was little more than a Mission village (**below**), becoming Mexican in 1821. Gold was found in 1848 and people from all over the world came to try their luck. At the same time, the US took possession of the West Coast. The Transcontinental Railroad helped to establish its financial base.

Exploratorium

MAP L6 ■ Pier 15, Embarcadero ■ (415) 528-4360 ■ Museum: open 10am–5pm Tue–Sun ■ Adm ■ www.exploratorium.edu

One of the world's first hands-on science museums, the Exploratorium now stands in a spectacular location on Pier 15. There are close to 600 exhibits that are spread among themed indoor galleries and a large outside space *(see p67)*. There are also educational programs, a theater, an interactive gift shop, a Bay Observatory, an outdoor plaza, and cafés.

Financial District

MAP M5

Montgomery Street, now the heart of the Financial District, was once lined with small shops where miners came to weigh their gold dust. It marks roughly the old shoreline of shallow Yerba Buena Cove, which was filled in during the Gold Rush to create more land. Today it is lined with banking "temples" of the early 20th century and modern fabrications of glass and steel. At the end of Market Street stands the renovated Ferry Building, which handled 100,000 commuters per day before the city's bridges were constructed, and is now a bustling meeting spot with cafés and artisan food shops. Its tower is inspired by the Moorish belfry of Seville's cathedral in Spain.

Jackson Square

MAP M5

This neighborhood by the Transamerica Pyramid *(see p50)* contains some of the city's oldest buildings. In the 19th century it was notorious for its squalor, and was nicknamed the "Barbary Coast," but brothels and drinking establishments have given way to offices and antiques shops. The blocks around Jackson Street and Hotaling Place feature many original facades.

Jackson Square plaque

Skyscrapers of the Financial District

Art on display in Union Square

⑨ Union Square
MAP P4

This important square, which gets its name from the pro-Union rallies held here in the early 1860s, has a $25-million upgraded look that includes performance spaces and grassy terraces. It is now the center for high-end shopping (see p79). With the Financial District on one side and the Theater District on the other, it is most picturesque along Powell Street, where the cable cars pass in front of the historic Westin St. Francis hotel (see p144). Its central column commemorates Admiral Dewey's victory at Manila Bay during the Spanish-American War of 1898.

⑩ Civic Center
MAP R1

The city's administrative center is an excellent example of Beaux Arts taste (see p50). It is perhaps the most elaborate city center complex in the US and it continues to be enhanced. Besides the imposing City Hall, with its vast rotunda and formal gardens, it also includes the War Memorial Opera House, the Louise M. Davies Symphony Hall (see p68), the Herbst Theater, the State Building, the new Main Library, and the old Main Library, which was re-inaugurated as the Asian Art Museum in 2003.

A WALK AROUND NORTH BEACH

▶ MORNING

Start at the top of North Beach, on **Telegraph Hill** (see p92), admire the famous views, and visit **Coit Tower** (see p50), making sure to take in the murals. Next, walk down to **Filbert Street** (see p92) and go right a couple of blocks until you get to lovely **Washington Square** (see p92), where, at **Saints Peter and Paul Catholic Church**, Marilyn Monroe and local baseball great Joe DiMaggio had their wedding pictures taken (see p92). Continue on along Columbus Avenue to the left and pay a visit to **Caffè Roma** (see p94), where you can indulge in a bit of people-watching. Or, just behind on Stockton Street, head to **Tony's Pizza Napoletana** (1570 Stockton St, (415) 835-9888), for award-winning pizza.

AFTERNOON

After lunch, take a left on Green Street and go over one block to **Upper Grant** (see p92), with its funky shops and bars, a regular hangout since the 1950s. Turn right on to Vallejo Street, where a visit to the famous **Caffè Trieste** (see p94) for a coffee and the authentic bohemian atmosphere is a must. Continue on down Columbus to William Saroyan Place and at No. 12 you'll find **Specs'**, an exuberant bar filled with Beat memorabilia. Finally, just across Columbus at No. 261 is the immortal **City Lights Bookstore** (see p92), where you can browse the Beat poetry written by owner Lawrence Ferlinghetti and friends.

North Beach Sights

Coit Tower mural

1 Coit Tower Murals
MAP L5

These frescoes were painted by local artists in 1934, to provide jobs during the Depression *(see p50)*. The murals give sociopolitical commentary yet are also appealing for their details of life in California at the time.

2 North Beach Views

The panoramic views from both the hill and the top of the Coit Tower are justly celebrated. The wide arc sweeping from the East Bay and the Bay Bridge to Alcatraz and the Golden Gate Bridge is breathtaking.

3 Telegraph Hill
MAP L5

Named after the semaphore installed on its crest in 1850. The hill's eastern side was dynamited to provide rocks for landfill. Steps descend its slopes, lined with gardens. At its summit is Coit Tower.

4 Broadway
MAP M5

Made famous in the 1960s for its various adult entertainments. The offerings haven't changed much, though today many venues are now more mainstream.

5 City Lights Bookstore
MAP M4 ■ 261 Columbus Ave
■ (415) 362-8193

The Beat poet Lawrence Ferlinghetti founded City Lights in 1953. It's a great place to leaf through a few volumes of poetry and the latest free papers to find out what's on.

6 Filbert Street Steps
MAP L5

The flowery descent down these steps provides great Bay views.

7 Upper Grant
MAP L4

Saloons, cafés, and bluesy music haunts give this northerly section of Grant Avenue a very alternative feel.

8 Caffè Trieste

If you're in the neighborhood on a Saturday afternoon, don't miss the spirited opera that takes place here. It is one of the longest-running musical shows in the city *(see p94)*.

9 Washington Square
MAP L4

This pretty park is lined with Italian bakeries, restaurants, and bars. Don't be surprised to see practitioners of tai chi doing their thing on the lawn every morning.

10 Saints Peter and Paul Church
MAP L4 ■ 666 Filbert St
■ Open daily

Neo-Gothic in conception, with an Italianesque facade, this church is also called the Italian Cathedral and the Fisherman's Church, since many Italians who originally lived in the neighborhood made their living by fishing *(see p48)*.

Saints Peter and Paul Church

Previous pages Alcatraz Island and the San Francisco skyline

Shops

Interior of Schein & Schein

1 Schein & Schein
MAP G2 ■ 1435 Grant Ave
■ (415) 399-8882

Antique maps and prints, rare books, fine engravings, and unique items fill this quaint shop, making it a great store for travel enthusiasts. The owner, Jimmie Schein, is a rich source of local history.

2 Arader Galleries
MAP M5 ■ 432 Jackson St, Jackson Square ■ (415) 788-5115

One of the most appealing shops in Jackson Square is like an art museum, featuring fine antique prints. You can marvel at treasures like Audubon's *Birds of America*, ancient maps, and historic prints.

3 Goorin Bros.
MAP L4 ■ 1612 Stockton St
■ (415) 402-0454

The city's finest hat shop for men and women prides itself on offering excellent service. Most of the custom hats are handmade in the US.

4 Little Vine
MAP P4 ■ 1541 Grant Ave
■ (415) 738-2221

Grab one of the sandwich specials sold here while browsing this quaint, European-inspired shop, filled with independently produced wines, artisan cheeses, pickles, and locally sourced honey.

5 Serge Sorokko Gallery
MAP P4 ■ 55 Geary St
■ (415) 421 7770

If you're in the market for a piece by one of the modern masters, this is an excellent place to browse important prints and other works by Picasso, Matisse, Miró, Chagall, and other 20th-century greats, such as Tapiès, Bacon, Twombly, and Warhol.

6 Christopher-Clark Fine Art
MAP P4 ■ 377 Geary St ■ (415) 397-7781

A gallery for modern European and American masters. A good stock of Bay Area artists, too.

7 Shreve & Co
MAP P4 ■ 117 Post St
■ (415) 421-2600

A San Francisco original and one of the most elegant jewelers to be found in the city. In addition to gems set in wonderful ways, you'll also find fine timepieces, Limoges porcelain, and Lalique crystal.

8 The North Face
MAP P4 ■ 180 Post St
■ (415) 433-3223

Originating in San Francisco, you'll find everything for the outdoor adventurer at this popular chain.

9 Macchiarini Creative Design
MAP G2 ■ 1544 Grant Ave
■ (415) 982-2229

The oldest ongoing arts design house, production studio, and gallery in the US, hand-crafting individually made sculptures and jewelry.

10 William Stout Architectural Books
MAP M4 ■ 804 Montgomery St
■ (415) 391-6757

A landmark for design buffs all over the world, this small shop is divided into two spaces, with newer books on display upstairs.

See map on p86

Cafés and Bars

Brightly painted and welcoming exterior of Caffè Trieste

1 Caffè Trieste
MAP M4 ▪ 609 Vallejo St
▪ (415) 982-2605

One of the most authentic cafés in
the city, rich with an arty sense of
nonchalance *(see p76)*.

2 Tosca Café
MAP M4 ▪ 242 Columbus Ave
▪ Closed L ▪ (415) 986-9651

Dating back to 1919, this North
Beach bar is a celebrity favorite.
The jukebox plays opera arias.

3 Caffè Roma
MAP L4 ▪ 526 Columbus Ave
▪ (415) 296-7942

You're as likely to hear Italian spoken
here as you are English. Caffè Roma
offers a friendly atmosphere in which
to people-watch whilst enjoying an
espresso, made with Lavazza beans.

4 Blue Bottle Café
MAP Q4 ▪ 66 Mint St ▪ (510)
653-3394

A cool, modern space known for its
hip crowd, and for turning out some
of the city's best coffee *(see p76)*.

5 Café de la Presse
MAP N5 ▪ 352 Grant Ave at
Sutter ▪ (415) 398-2680

This small corner café carries an
impressive assortment of international newspapers, and style and
design magazines. Grab a table
and just watch the world go by.

6 Royal Exchange
MAP N6 ▪ 301 Sacramento St
▪ (415) 956-1710

For a proper beer and burger, head
to this classic watering hole, which
has more than 30 beers on tap.

7 Le Colonial
MAP N3 ▪ 20 Cosmo Place
▪ (415) 931-3600

This 1920s-style bar serves
Vietnamese-French food and fancy
cocktails in a tropical setting. It is
always busy – from its happy hour
until the early hours.

8 Church Key
MAP L4 ▪ 1402 Grant Ave at
Green St ▪ (415) 963-1713

This Victorian-themed bar has
one of the largest beer selections
in San Francisco.

9 Bix
MAP M5 ▪ 56 Gold St between
Montgomery & Sansome ▪ (415)
433-6300

Tucked into a Downtown alley,
this sultry supper club features
potent cocktails and smooth jazz.

10 Press Club
MAP P4 ▪ 20 Yerba Buena Lane
at Market ▪ (415) 744-5000

This popular and ultramodern
lounge offers a wide selection of
wines, as well as a specially-crafted
menu of food accompaniments.

Places to Eat

PRICE CATEGORIES
For a three-course meal for one with half a bottle of wine (or equivalent meal), taxes, and extra charges.

$ under $40 $$ $40–$80 $$$ over $80

1 Kokkari Estiatorio

MAP M6 ■ 200 Jackson St ■ (415) 981-0983 ■ $$

The Greek cuisine here is a delectable revelation of flavors. The lamb shank and grilled octopus are not to be missed.

2 La Mar

MAP M6 ■ Pier 1.5 Embarcadero at Washington ■ (415) 397-8880 ■ $$

Situated on the waterfront, this restaurant serves innovative Peruvian seafood *(see p74)*.

3 One Market

MAP N6 ■ 1 Market St at Steuart ■ (415) 777-5577 ■ Closed Sun ■ $$

The views of the Bay's lights from here are spectacular at night, and the farm-fresh food is memorable.

4 Sears Fine Food

MAP P4 ■ 439 Powell St ■ (415) 986-0700/1160 ■ $

This 1950s retro coffee shop is famous for its breakfasts, and is always a reliable choice for a quick fill-up *(see p77)*.

Sears Fine Food

5 Quince

MAP M5 ■ 470 Pacific Ave ■ (415) 775-8500 ■ Closed L ■ $$

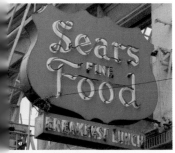

The northern Italian cuisine, made with local ingredients, has earned rave reviews for this Michelin-starred restaurant *(see p74)*.

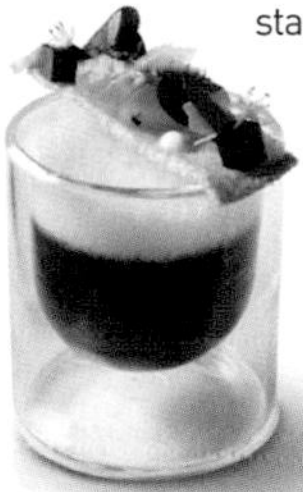

Grapefruit mousse, Quince

6 Lers Ros Thai

MAP K2 ■ 730 Larkin St ■ (415) 931-6917 ■ $

This restaurant lives up to it's name – in Sanskrit, 'lers' translates as excellent and 'rost' means 'taste' *(see p75)*.

7 Gitane

MAP P4 ■ 6 Claude Lane at Sutter ■ (415) 788-6686 ■ Closed L ■ $$

Gypsy chic meets classic Iberian cuisine at this popular restaurant, located on a charming cobbled alley *(see p74)*.

8 Sotto Mare

MAP L4 ■ 552 Green St ■ (415) 398-3181 ■ $$

Housed in a 19th-century building, Sotto Mare serves Italian seafood dishes. Don't miss the crab *cioppino*.

9 Tadich Grill

MAP N5 ■ 240 California St ■ (415) 391-1849 ■ $$

Beginning as a coffee stand in 1849, today this traditional restaurant serves classics such as clam chowder. Brusque staff add some fun to the atmosphere. No reservations required.

10 Yank Sing

MAP H2 ■ 101 Spear St ■ (415) 781-1111 ■ $$

Head to the busy Rincon Center in SoMA for excellent Chinese cuisine. Yank Sing is famous for its signature Shanghai dumplings, with over 60 varieties on offer.

See map on p86

⭐10 The North Shoreline

San Francisco began to grow along the North Shoreline when the Spanish set up a military outpost at the Presidio in 1776. Today the shoreline is a showcase of both historical and modern attractions. The Palace of Fine Arts recalls the 1915 Panama-Pacific International Exposition; the vintage homes of the Marina District have stellar Bay views; ships depart from Pier 41 for Bay cruises; and tourists crowd the stores and seafood eateries of Fisherman's Wharf. Walk all the way from the Golden Gate Bridge to the Embarcadero to get a sense of the many eras of the "Paris of the West."

Embarcadero street sign

1 Angel and Treasure Islands

Ferries from Pier 41

A trip out to Angel Island, which is now a state park, can mean a day of picnicking, biking, hiking, kayaking, or swimming. But in the early 1900s it was the "Ellis Island of the West," where would-be immigrants, mostly Chinese, could be detained for months on end. During World War II, it served as a prisoner of war camp and then later as a missile base. Treasure Island was built in 1939 for the Golden Gate International Exposition and served as a US Navy base during

World War II. It is now once again owned by the city of San Francisco and is one of its suburbs.

2 Golden Gate Bridge

This renowned masterpiece of engineering sets off the entrance to San Francisco Bay in a spectacular way. It never fails to awe both first-timers and old-timers alike. Walking or cycling across its length is an unforgettable experience *(see pp12–13)*.

3 Alcatraz

America's "Devil's Island" didn't operate as a prison for a part-

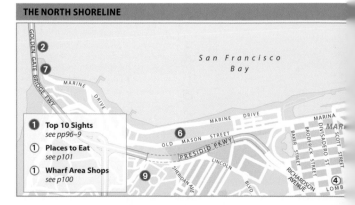

THE NORTH SHORELINE

San Francisco Bay

1 Top 10 Sights
see pp96–9

① Places to Eat
see p101

① Wharf Area Shops
see p100

Alcatraz as seen from the prison gardens

icularly long time, but the cell blocks and control room can still manage to evoke a chill *(see pp18–21)*.

4 Fisherman's Wharf
Although now largely tourist-oriented, there are still authentic maritime sights to see, aromas to savor, and salt air to breathe along these piers. Pier 39 is a highlight, with its various amusements, shops, and restaurants *(see pp16–17)*.

5 The Embarcadero
MAP G1

Skirted with palm trees, the Embarcadero runs from the North Shoreline down to the coast of Downtown, from Pier 45 to the San Francisco Giants' AT&T Park. It is lined with attractions and departure points for cruise ships. The Alcatraz Landing is at Pier 33 and Hornblower Cruises leaves from Pier 3. Scenic views can be enjoyed at the pedestrianized piers 7 and 14. On the south waterfront, you'll find the 60-ft- (18-m-) tall *Cupid's Span*. It is a simple sculpture of the god's bow and arrow, which is half buried in the ground. It perfectly represents the city's romantic reputation. Piers north of the Ferry Building have odd numbers, while those to the south have even numbers.

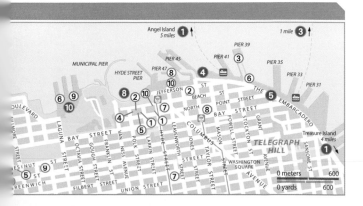

The Golden Gate Bridge viewed from Crissy Field

6 Crissy Field
MAP D1

Originally marshland and dunes, the field was filled in for the 1915 Panama-Pacific Exposition and paved over for use as an airfield by the army from 1919 to 1936. With the establishment of the Presidio as a national park under the supervision of the city, a massive restoration project has returned part of Crissy Field to wetlands and the rest to lawns, pathways, and picnic areas. The city's over 4 million-sq ft (370,000-sq m) "Front Yard" is one of the prime viewing sites for the Fourth of July fireworks. Extending over 4-miles (7-km), the Golden Gate Promenade is a paved pathway that runs through this district from Aquatic Park to Fort Point.

7 Fort Point
MAP C1

Crashing waves, passing ships, and windsurfers, along with a Civil War-era fort loaded with cannons, guns, and other military artifacts, make for spectacular photos here beneath the Golden Gate Bridge (see p12). You can fish along the seawall and take self-guided or ranger-led tours to learn about the building of the bridge. At the foot of the cliffs on the western side of the fort is a small beach loved by nude sun worshippers.

Disney museum exhibit, the Presidio

8 Aquatic Park
MAP F1 ■ Visitor Center: 499 Jefferson St ■ (415) 447-5000 ■ Open 9:30am–5pm daily

Within the sheltering arm of a curved fishing pier is the warmest, safest Bayside beach. The shallow water is fine for wading and swimming, although it is dependably cold. Joggers and bikers love the paved trail. The cable car turnaround is steps away at Beach and Hyde Streets. In the park you will find a Visitor Center and the Maritime Museum (see p53).

9 The Presidio
MAP D2

This wooded corner of the city has stunning views over the Golden Gate. From 1776 until 1994, it was occupied by first the Spanish, then

EARTHQUAKE! THE LANDFILL PROBLEM

Most of the Marina area, as well as the majority of the Financial District, was built on landfill. As time has proven, this was not such a good idea in a seismically active zone. When the Loma Prieta earthquake struck at 5:04pm on October 17, 1989, all such landfills liquefied, gas mains fractured, and several Marina homes slid off their foundations. Buildings that withstand best are those built on bedrock, which includes most of the inland areas of the city.

the Mexican, and finally, the US armies. It is now a major part of the Golden Gate National Recreational Area. It is full of nature trails, streams, forests, drives, and historic structures. Also here is the Walt Disney Family Museum, which gives insight into Walt Disney's life through photographs, animation, and a range of interactive exhibits.

The waterfront by Fort Mason Center

⑩ Fort Mason Center
MAP F1

Since 1976 some of the buildings at this Civil War-era military base have been devoted to cultural programs. Some 50 cultural organizations now call it home. Among the most prominent are the Mexican Museum, the Museo Italo Americano *(see p55)*, the Long Now Foundation, SFMOMA Artists Gallery, the Children's Art Center, the Magic Theatre *(see p69)*, and Herbst Pavilion. The city's finest vegetarian restaurant, Greens, is also here, enjoying views of the Bay *(see p74)*.

A BIKE RIDE THROUGH THE PRESIDIO

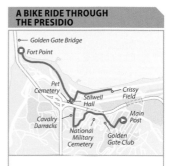

▶ Beginning at the Visitor Information Center, where you can pick up an excellent map, first explore the **Main Post**. Here you can ride around the Parade Ground and see the earliest surviving buildings of the Presidio, dating from the 1860s, as well as 18th-century Spanish adobe wall fragments in the former Officers' Club.

Exit the area on Sheridan Avenue, which takes you past the Spanish Colonial Revival-style **Golden Gate Club**, and turn left onto Lincoln Boulevard, which winds its way around the **National Military Cemetery**. Turn right on McDowell Avenue; on the left you will see the Colonial Revival **Cavalry Barracks**.

Now go past the five brick Stables, off to both the left and the right, and stop at the quirky **Pet Cemetery** on the left, where guard dogs are buried as well as many family pets. Next, head under Highway 101 to encounter **Stilwell Hall**, built in 1921 as enlisted barracks and a mess hall for the airmen. Turn left to take in the metal Aerodrome Hangars from the same era, then proceed on to **Crissy Field** to admire the views.

Double back at this point to take the next left down toward the Bay itself and join the Golden Gate Promenade all the way out to **Fort Point**. As long as the fog is not too bad, this is the perfect spot to experience the awe-inspiring **Golden Gate Bridge** *(see pp12–13)* and the crashing waves of the mighty Pacific.

See map on pp96–7 ←

Fisherman's Wharf Area Shops

1 Ghirardelli Chocolate
MAP K2 ■ Ghirardelli Square, 900 North Point St ■ (415) 447-2846

Stop by for a free sample and then stock up on your mouthwatering favorites. Take home some chocolate cable cars.

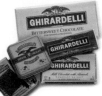

Ghirardelli Chocolate

2 Gigi + Rose
MAP K2 ■ Ghirardelli Square, 900 North Point St ■ (415) 765-9060

Quirky souvenirs, accessories, and children's outfits, many of which are designed by the owners, are for sale.

3 Alcatraz Gift Shop
MAP J4 ■ 2nd level, Pier 39 ■ (415) 249-4666

Souvenirs of the Rock, from tin cups to prisoner outfits are for sale here. Photos and history books can be found at the Alcatraz Book Store on Pier 41.

4 Lola of North Beach
MAP K2 ■ Ghirardelli Square, 900 North Point St ■ (415) 567-7760

There is a wonderful souvenir section, stationery, and locally designed glassware and ornaments at this gift shop.

5 Jackson & Polk
MAP K2 ■ Ghirardelli Square, 900 North Point St ■ (415) 345-9708

A little bit of everything is on offer in this boutique of books and treasures, which prides itself on offering a wide selection of San Francisco-based brands.

6 NFL Shop
MAP J4 ■ PIER 39, Ground Level ■ (415) 397-2027

This shop is officially licensed to sell products for all major league sports, so this is your chance to stock up on the jerseys, caps, and other merchandise of all your favorite teams.

7 Patagonia
MAP J4 ■ 770 North Point St ■ (415) 771-2050

The San Francisco store of this quintessentially Californian company sells classic fleeces and outdoor wear. One percent of annual sales is donated to environmental charities.

8 Cost Plus World Market
MAP K3 ■ 2552 Taylor St ■ (415) 928-6200

The original import market that set the trend for all the others. It can still surprise with a well-chosen item from some faraway land.

9 Book Bay Fort Mason
MAP F1 ■ Fort Mason Center, Building C ■ (415) 771-1076

Great secondhand books, records, and CDs, with all the proceeds supporting programs in San Francisco's libraries. You won't find better prices anywhere else.

10 Frank's Fisherman Supply
MAP E1 ■ 366 Jefferson St ■ (415) 775-1165

Frank's has been selling ship models, rare navigation devices, paintings, marine antiques, and various historic ship paraphernalia since 1946.

Merchandise at Jackson & Polk

Places to Eat

PRICE CATEGORIES
For a three course meal for one with half
a bottle of wine (or equivalent meal),
taxes, and extra charges.
....
$ under $40 $$ $40–$80 $$$ over $80

1 Gary Danko
MAP K2 ▪ 800 North Point
St at Hyde ▪ (415) 749-2060 ▪ $$$
The French-American menu served
here allows you to create your own
fixed-price selection. If you don't
have a reservation (which are taken
up to two months in advance), head
for the bar, where you can order
anything on the menu.

Interior of Gary Danko restaurant

2 The Codmother
MAP J4 ▪ 496 Beach St ▪ (415)
606-9349 ▪ Closed D ▪ $
This food truck serves outstanding
fish tacos, fish and chips, and
assorted chip-shop desserts,
such as fried Oreos.

3 Isa
MAP E2 ▪ 3324 Steiner St
between Chestnut & Lombard ▪ (415)
567-9588 ▪ Closed L ▪ $$
At this tiny Marina restaurant, the
concept is Nouvelle French tapas,
with small plates such as honey-
spiced calamari and lobster broth
sprinkled with tarragon.

4 A16
MAP E1 ▪ 2355 Chestnut St
▪ (415) 771-2216 ▪ $$
An authentic southern Italian
dining experience that's worth
getting dressed up for (see p74).

Exterior of the popular Tacolicious

5 Tacolicious
MAP K4 ▪ 2031 Chestnut St
▪ (415) 649-6077 ▪ $$
A multitude of taco choices are
served at this popular joint. Enjoy the
free chips and salsa while you wait.

6 Greens
MAP F1 ▪ Fort Mason Center,
Buchanan St, Building A ▪ (415)
771-6222 ▪ $$
Since 1979, the inventive vegetarian
dishes and Bayside panoramas here
have delighted patrons (see p74).

7 Zarzuela
MAP L2 ▪ 2000 Hyde St
▪ (415) 346-0800 ▪ Closed L, Sun &
Mon ▪ $$
Delicious, well-priced tapas is
served up in this cozy restaurant.

8 Scoma's
MAP J2 ▪ Pier 47 on Al Scoma
Way ▪ (415) 771-4383 ▪ $$
A Fisherman's Wharf (see pp16–17)
seafood tradition since 1965. Enjoy
the cracked crab roasted in garlic.

9 Zushi Puzzle
MAP F2 ▪ 1910 Lombard St
▪ (415) 931-9319 ▪ Closed L ▪ $$
One of the city's best sushi spots,
thanks to its fresh fish and friendly chef.

10 The Buena Vista Café
MAP K2 ▪ 2765 Hyde St
▪ (415) 474-5044 ▪ $
This café claims to have invented
Irish coffee. The menu features
classic American dishes.

See map on pp96–7 ←

TOP 10 Central Neighborhoods

Haight Street sign

As is the case with most parts of San Francisco, diversity is the keynote here. This area encompasses the oldest money and the highest society of the founding families of the city, as well as some of its poorest citizens. It takes in the staunchest pillars of the politically savvy. True conservatives are a rarity in this progressive city, but you will find them here alongside the wildest let-it-all-hang-out freethinkers. There's a considerable swath of the comfortably middle-class here too who, like most San Franciscans, are simply intent on enjoying the beauties and pleasures of their great city.

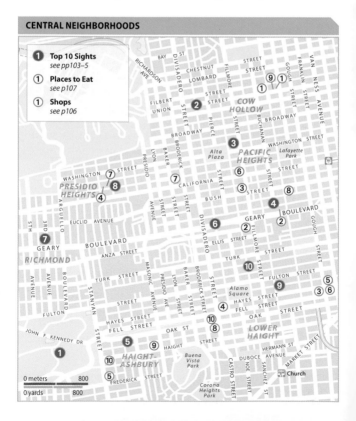

CENTRAL NEIGHBORHOODS

1 **Top 10 Sights**
see pp103–5

1 **Places to Eat**
see p107

1 **Shops**
see p106

Grand facades of Pacific Heights

1 Golden Gate Park

One of the largest and finest parks-cum-cultural centers in the world. No visit to the city is complete without taking in some of its wonders *(see pp24–5)*.

2 Union Street
MAP E2

A neighborhood shopping artery loaded with tradition, Union Street is noted for its sidewalk cafés, bookstores, and designer boutiques, housed in converted Victorian charmers. The street is at the heart of the Cow Hollow neighborhood, whose name recalls its previous life as a dairy pasture *(see p79)*.

3 Pacific Heights
MAP E2

A grander, more exclusive residential area is hard to imagine. Commanding as it does heights of up to 300 ft (100 m) overlooking the magnificent Bay, everything about it proclaims power and wealth. The blocks between Alta Plaza and Lafayette parks are the very heart of the area, but the grandeur extends from Gough to Divisadero Street and beyond. On a sunny day, there's nothing

more exhilarating than scaling its hills and taking in the perfectly manicured streets, the to-die-for views, and the palatial dwellings. The Spreckels Mansion, a limestone palace in the Beaux Arts tradition, on Washington and Octavia Streets, is the brightest gem of the lot, now owned by the novelist Danielle Steel.

4 Japantown
MAP F3

This neighborhood has been the focus of the Japanese community since the early 20th century. The Japan Center was built as part of an ambitious 1960s plan to revitalize the Fillmore District. Blocks of aging Victorian buildings were demolished and replaced by the Geary Expressway and this Japanese-style shopping complex with a five-tiered, 75-ft (22-m) Peace Pagoda at its heart. *Taiko* drummers perform here during the Cherry Blossom Festival each April *(see p82)*. The extensive malls are lined with authentic Japanese shops and restaurants, plus an eight-screen cinema, and the Kabuki Springs and Spa. More shops and restaurants can be found along the outdoor mall across Post Street.

Japantown Peace Pagoda

FLOWER POWER

In 1967, San Francisco witnessed the Summer of Love *(see p43)*, including a 75,000-strong Human Be-In at Golden Gate Park. People were drawn here – many with flowers in their hair – by the acid-driven melodies of Jefferson Airplane, Janis Joplin, Jimi Hendrix, and The Doors. Love was free, concerts were free, drugs were free, even food and healthcare were free. Soon, however, public alarm, and too many bad trips, caused the bubble to burst. In 2017, a variety of special events and exhibitions were held throughout the city to celebrate the 50th anniversary of the Summer of Love.

5 Haight-Ashbury
MAP D4

This anarchic quarter is one of the most scintillating and unconventional in the city, resting firmly on its laurels as ground zero for the worldwide Flower-Power explosion of the 1960s *(see p43)*. Admire the beautiful old Queen Anne-style houses, a few of them still painted in the psychedelic pigments of the hippie era, as well as the unique shops and the venerable Haight-Ashbury Free Clinic. The Lower Haight is noted for its edgy clubs and bars.

Holy Virgin Cathedral, Richmond District

Geary Boulevard

6 Geary Boulevard
MAP F3

One of the city's main traffic arteries, sweeping from Van Ness all the way out to Cliff House, Geary Boulevard is a typically unprepossessing and functional urban thoroughfare. It begins its journey at Market Street, sweeps past Union Square, and then forms the heart of the Theater District, before venturing into the notorious Tenderloin, home to seedy clubs. After it crosses Van Ness, it zips past Japantown and the funky Fillmore District. Soon you're in the Richmond District and before you know it, there's the Pacific Ocean.

7 The Richmond District
MAP C3

This flat district of row houses begins at Masonic Street, sandwiched between Golden Gate Park and California Street. It ultimately extends all the way to the Pacific Ocean, being more and more prone to stay fog-bound the farther west you go. The district is very ethnically diverse and generally middle class. Over the decades, it has been settled by Russians, East European Jews, and latterly Chinese-Americans and another wave of Russians.

8 Presidio Heights
MAP D3

Originally part of the "Great Sand Waste" to the west, this neighborhood is now one of the most elite of all.

The zone centers on Sacramento Street as its discreet shopping area. It's worth a stroll, primarily for the architecture. Of interest are the Swedenborgian Church at 2107 Lyon Street, the Roos House at 3500 Jackson Street, and Temple Emanu-El at 2 Lake Street.

⑨ Hayes Valley
MAP F4

Rising like a phoenix from the ashes of racial unrest in what used to be a rundown African-American slum, this small area has now become one of San Francisco's hipper shopping and dining districts. The dismantling of an ugly freeway overpass following the 1989 earthquake helped turn the tide, and the welcome result is a chic area that hasn't lost its edge. Hayes Valley festivals take place in midsummer, when the area's streets are thronged with revelers.

Alamo Square, Western Addition

⑩ Western Addition
MAP E3

This area, too, was once sandy waste, but after World War II the district became populated by Southern African-Americans who came west for work. For a short time, it was famous for jazz and blues clubs, as embodied, until his death in 2001, by John Lee Hooker and his Boom Boom Room. Today, it is still largely African-American in character and rather rundown, although it does include the architecturally odd Cathedral of St. Mary of the Assumption (see p48) and photogenic Alamo Square (see p51).

A HIPPIE TOUR OF HAIGHT-ASHBURY

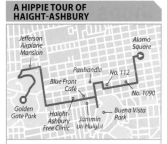

▶ **MORNING**

Begin at **Alamo Square** (see p51), with the Westerfeld House at 1198 Fulton at Scott, former residence of Ken Kesey, the writer and visionary who arguably got the whole 1960s movement going. Walk up Scott, turn right on Page and go to **No. 1090**, where the rock band Big Brother and the Holding Company got their start. A block and a half farther on, go right on Lyon to **No. 122**, where Janis Joplin lived for most of 1967 (see p45).

Continue on to the **Panhandle**, an extension of Golden Gate Park, where in June 1967 the Jimi Hendrix Experience gave a free concert. Now turn left on Central and head up to steep **Buena Vista Park**, site of public Love-Ins in the 1960s and 1970s. Turn right on Haight and check out **Jammin On Haight** (1400 Haight Street at Masonic), which is one of the fanciest hippie shops.

Continue on to the Haight-Ashbury intersection and walk along Haight to Clayton; at No. 558 is the much-loved **Haight-Ashbury Free Clinic**, still imbued with the spirit of the 1960s. If you are hungry, stop in for a snack at **Blue Front Café** (see p107).

Refreshed, walk towards Golden Gate Park, then turn right on Stanyan all the way to Fulton. At 2400 Fulton stands the former Jefferson Airplane Mansion, which used to be painted black. Finally, head into **Golden Gate Park** (see pp24–5) and make your way to the drum circles on Hippie Hill to groove to the tribal beats.

See map on p102

Shops

Clothes on sale at Marmalade

1 Marmalade
MAP F2 ■ 1843 Union St
■ (415) 757-8614

A chic yet casual boutique with dresses, tops, and jewelry that are stylish but not overpriced. Marmalade also sells fabulous bags, trinkets, and other great gift items.

2 Daiso Japan
MAP F3 ■ 22 Peace Plaza
■ (415) 359-9397

Discount store selling Japanese household items, snacks, and other fun imports.

3 Dark Garden
MAP F4 ■ 321 Linden St
■ (415) 431-7684

Popular shop for women's couture and locally-made, custom, and ready-to-wear corsets, dresses, and wedding gowns. Famous clients include Christina Aguilera and Dita Von Teese.

4 Dottie Doolittle
MAP D3 ■ 3680 Sacramento St
■ (415) 673-1334

A long-established mainstay, this high-end clothier carries fashionable American and European labels for babies and kids up to the age of 12.

5 Past Perfect
MAP D4 ■ 854 Stanyan St
■ (415) 418-6754

There is tons to choose from at this huge, fairly-priced vintage store. Plan to spend a while perusing their unique furniture, lighting, and art – there is something for everyone here. The staff are friendly, too.

6 Polanco
MAP F4 ■ 334 Gough St
■ (415) 252-5753

A sophisticated gallery of Mexican arts, which features silver jewelry, colorful Day of the Dead masks and crafts, as well as the work of emerging Mexican artists.

7 Sue Fisher King
MAP F2 ■ 3067 Sacramento St
■ (415) 922-7276

In 1978, Sue Fisher King opened her shop of trinkets and treasures for the home, fine jewelry, and divinely scented bath products. Today, it's still considered one of the city's must-visits.

8 Comix Experience
MAP E4 ■ 305 Divisadero St
■ (415) 863-9258

The comics here have adult aficionados in mind: *The Ring of the Nibelung*, *The Filth*, *Naughty Bits*, and *Static-X* are just a few examples of the wacky titles that await you in both new and vintage issues.

9 Chronicle Books
MAP F4 ■ 1846 Union St
■ (415) 345-8435

More of a gift shop than a true bookstore, Chronicle Books is also a publisher and stocks its own titles. The store offers a large number of unconventional books, as well as gorgeous cookbooks, and a wide selection of gifts.

10 Amoeba Music
MAP D4 ■ 1855 Haight St
■ (415) 831-1200

Besides thousands of LPs, tapes, and CDs, there's also a huge selection of DVDs and posters at this record store, which is part of an independent chain, and prides itself on being the world's largest independent music store.

Places to Eat

PRICE CATEGORIES
For a three-course meal for one with half
a bottle of wine (or equivalent meal),
taxes, and extra charges.

$ under $40 **$$** $40–$80 **$$$** over $80

German chocolate
cake at Absinthe

1 Perry's
MAP F2 ▪ 1944 Union St
▪ (415) 922-9022 ▪ $

A San Francisco institution, noted for
its burgers and other all-American
favorites, including meatloaf, prime
rib, and fried chicken.

2 State Bird Provisions
MAP F3 ▪ 1529 Fillmore St
▪ (415) 795-1272 ▪ $$

A trendy Michelin-starred restaurant
serving small plates of French and
American food. Choose most of your
food from a cart or tray of dishes
brought out by the waiting staff.

3 SPQR
MAP E3 ▪ 1911 Fillmore St
▪ (415) 771-7779 ▪ $$

Reservations are accepted online
only at this no-frills, rustic Roman-
inspired eatery with mouthwatering
antipasti and superior service.

4 Nopa
MAP E4 ▪ 560 Divisadero St
▪ (415) 864 8643 ▪ Closed L ▪ $

Considered one of the best
restaurants in the city, Nopa
has a seasonally changing menu.

Interior of Nopa

5 Absinthe
MAP F4 ▪ 398 Hayes St
▪ (415) 551-1590 ▪ $$

This Parisian-style bistro serves
specials such as the extremely
popular *foie gras torchon*.

6 Pizzeria Delfina
MAP F5 ▪ 2406 California St
▪ (415) 440-1189 ▪ $

Rustic, simple, and fresh, this
popular pizzeria serves incredible
Neapolitan thin-crust pizzas in
addition to delicious, authentic
antipasti and salami.

7 Spruce
MAP D3 ▪ 3640 Sacramento St
▪ (415) 931-5100 ▪ $$$

Ranked among the "Top 100
Restaurants", this eatery offers a seasonal meat-focused menu *(see p75)*.

8 Kiss Seafood
MAP F3 ▪ 1700 Laguna St
▪ (415) 474-2866 ▪ $$

Book ahead to eat delectable sushi
and sashimi at this tiny restaurant.

9 Blue Front Café
MAP E4 ▪ 1430 Haight St
▪ (415) 252-5917 ▪ $

For cheap, tasty Mediterranean
wraps and sandwiches, this café
is a local favorite.

10 Nopalito
MAP H3 ▪ 306 Broderick St at
Oak ▪ (415) 437-0303 ▪ $

A fresh take on Mexican street food –
everything served here is organic,
from the *mole* (sauces) to *pozole*
(soups). The mescal and tequila
cocktails are unforgettable *(see p74)*.

See map on p102

🔟 Southern Neighborhoods

The southern part of San Francisco comprises some of the liveliest, most authentic parts of the city – the clubs of SoMa, the gay world of the Castro, and the Latino Mission District. There are also some up-and-coming neighborhoods on this side of the city, such as Bernal Heights and Glen Park, as the more central areas have priced creative types out toward the southern borders. Laid-back Noe Valley was the first such choice for high-rent refugees, but it, too, has become gentrified and pushed people farther south.

Mission Dolores facade detail

SOUTHERN NEIGHBORHOODS

- ① **Top 10 Sights** see pp109–11
- ① **Places to Eat** see p115
- ① **Shops** see p112
- ① **Bars** see p114
- ① **Nightclubs** see p113

1 China Basin
MAP H4

This old shipping port has not been exempt from the upsurge of interest in previously neglected areas. The main change has been wrought by the building of the AT&T Park, home to the San Francisco Giants, the city's major league baseball team, and developers have

China Basin statue

already put forth ideas for putting the zone to use. A number of restaurants, bars, and clubs, many with port views, have opened up here or have been refurbished.

2 Mission Dolores
MAP F5 ▪ 3321 16th St at Dolores St ▪ (415) 621-8203
▪ Open 9am–4pm daily
▪ www.mission dolores.org

The Spanish Misión San Francisco de Asís, from which the city takes its name, is a marvel of preservation and atmospheric charm. It was founded in 1776, a few weeks before the Declaration of Independence.

3 South of Market
MAP R4

This former rough-and-tumble warehouse district now houses high-tech offices. Some of the city's best eateries, bars, and galleries are in SoMa (see p35).

4 Castro District
MAP E5

This neighborhood, with the landmark Castro Theatre, is the center of San Francisco's gay community. The intersection of Castro and 18th Streets is known as the "Gayest Four Corners of the World." This openly homosexual nexus emerged in the 1970s as a pilgrimage for gay travelers from all over the world. Every Halloween, Castro Street hosts a costume party and parade that is second to the San Francisco Pride parade (see pp82–3).

Castro Theatre

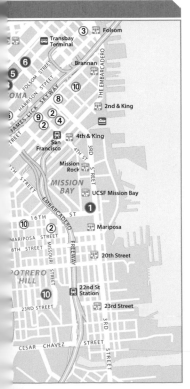

A GAY CITY

After the free-love movement of the 1960s (see p104), homosexuals realized that they had rights to stand up for. They started moving into the Castro in the 1970s. In no time, the neighborhood was a nonstop – and unstoppable – party of freewheeling sexual excess. Suddenly gays were "out" in their legions, which brought with it political clout. San Francisco is still one of the easiest places in the world to live an openly gay lifestyle.

Yerba Buena Center

This is fast becoming one of San Francisco's leading centers for the performing arts and has a growing number of museums representing the city's ethnic diversity. Every year sees some new addition to the complex (see pp34–5).

6 San Francisco Museum of Modern Art

San Francisco's home for its extensive modern art collection is as impressive outside as it is awe-inspiring inside. Its expansive galleries enable a great amount of its stunning treasure of paintings, photography, media and digital installations, designs, and sculptures to be on show (see pp32–3).

7 Noe Valley
MAP E6

Once a simple working-class neighborhood, until the 1970s brought hippies, gays, and artists to its slopes and Noe Valley became an attractive alternative to more established quarters. In its heyday it was known as both "Nowhere Valley" for its relative remoteness, and as "Granola Valley" for its nature-loving denizens. Lately, it has been taken over by middle-class professionals, who value it for its orderliness, but 24th Street still hums with activity and it is lined with cafés and bookstores.

8 Moscone Center

Embellishing the SoMa cultural and business district, the Moscone Center (see p34) consists of an impressive central building, as well as a new, glass-enclosed expansion. The city's largest convention space also boasts an arrival plaza, enclosed bridges, and gardens, all connecting the massive three-block facility to surrounding hotels, theaters, restaurants, museums, and parks.

9 Mission District
MAP F5

The Mission is home to many of San Francisco's Latinos. They have brought their culture with them – *taquerías,*

San Francisco Museum of Modern Art

salsa clubs, Santería shops, murals, and Spanish are found everywhere. Its festivals are not to be missed, especially Carnaval *(see p82)*.

Carnaval parade, Mission District

⑩ Potrero Hill
MAP H5 ■ Anchor Brewing Co, 1705 Mariposa St ■ (415) 863-8350 ■ www.anchorbrewing.com

This SoMa hill was once set to become the next big thing, but its isolation kept that from happening, cut off from the rest of the city, as it is, by freeways on three sides and its own precipitous inclines. It has remained a quiet neighborhood with spectacular views. There are restaurants, bars, and many design stores here, but it is mostly residential. A noteworthy site is the Anchor Brewing Company. For $15 per person, you can participate in a tour and tasting session. There are only two tours each weekday; you must phone to book.

A WALK AROUND THE CASTRO DISTRICT

Church Street Muni Station
Harvey Milk Plaza
The Cafe
Twin Peaks
Badlands
Castro Theater
Moby Dick
Brand X Antiques

▶ Begin at the gay mecca of San Francisco, the **Church Street Muni Station** on Upper Market. Decades ago, this corner became the symbolic starting point of the Castro neighborhood, but it is on the next block, between Sanchez and Noe, that the gay shops and venues really begin to proliferate. Towards the corner of Castro is **The Cafe** at 2369 Market, offering a range of strong drinks accompanied by Top 40 mixes.

Continuing on to Castro Street, take in **Harvey Milk Plaza**, with its huge rainbow flag; the plaza is named after the slain gay leader *(see p47)*. On the opposite corner, check out **Twin Peaks** *(see p73)* at 401 Castro, the oldest totally "out" gay bar, which is notable for its picture windows affording a full view of goings-on, both from inside and outside.

Pushing on to No. 429, allow the **Castro Theatre** to capture your attention. One of the city's most ornate cinema palaces, it hosts innumerable premieres of gay-themed films. Farther along at No. 570, **Brand X Antiques** *(see p112)* is a great place to browse, with its eclectic collection of goods, ranging from furniture to homoerotica. One block over, on Hartford Street, **Moby Dick** *(see p72)* is a popular spot that attracts a steady crowd of regulars. Stop here to shoot some pool or pinball while enjoying 1980s tunes.

Finally, just up 18th Street at No. 4121 is **Badlands** *(see p73)*, which is always full of the cool set, especially after 10pm.

See map on pp108–9 ←

Shops

1 **Needles & Pens**
MAP F5 ▪ 1173 Valencia St
▪ (415) 255-1534

There's a little bit of everything at this funky, eclectic store. Don't miss the fantastic magazine selection, unique cards, stationery, and T-shirts, as well as the gallery.

2 **440 Brannan Studio Showroom**
MAP R6 ▪ 440 Brannan St
▪ (415) 348-0000

Limited production clothing for men and women, made on-site by local, talented designers. Watch your shirt being sewed in the factory at the back.

3 **Borderlands Books**
MAP F5 ▪ 866 Valencia St
▪ (415) 824-8203

A bookstore specializing in science fiction, horror, and fantasy. Whether these genres are your cup of tea or not, Borderlands is worth a visit for a dose of the unusual.

4 **Brand X Antiques**
MAP E5 ▪ 570 Castro St
▪ (415) 626-8908

The gay couple who own this shop share a discerning and humorous eye for antiques. In addition to baubles, rings, and furniture, the collection also features tongue-in-cheek vintage homoerotica.

5 **The Voyager Shop**
MAP F5 ▪ 365 Valencia St
▪ (415) 779-2712

A unique retail store of worldwide treasures, with everything from clothing and accessories to stationery and ocean gear – and a full gallery to boot.

6 **Paxton Gate**
MAP F5 ▪ 824 Valencia St
▪ (415) 824-1872

This wonderland of unique items for gifts and home decor even includes strange pieces of taxidermy. Kids will love this place as much as adults do.

7 **Astrid's Rabat Shoes**
MAP F6 ▪ 3909 24th St
▪ (415) 282-7400

If walking the steep city streets is challenging your footwear, this Noe Valley store can fit you with a new pair of sturdy and stylish, walking shoes.

8 **City Art Gallery**
MAP F5 ▪ 828 Valencia St
▪ (415) 970-9900

This gallery sells work from dozens of local artists in a variety of media. Much of it is reasonably priced, making it a great spot to find a unique gift.

9 **Alexander Book Company**
MAP P5 ▪ 50 Second St
▪ (415) 495-2992

Located near the Montgomery Street BART station, this library has three floors of all genres of literature, from children's books and classics, to coffee-table books and textbooks.

10 **Fatto a Mano**
MAP G4 ▪ 129 Carolina St
▪ (415) 525-4348

Owned by a husband-and-wife team, this store sells unique home furnishings, including ceramics, glassware, and kitchen accessories. Their beautiful handmade furnishings are imported from Italy.

Treasures and taxidermy, Paxton Gate

Nightclubs

 The Stud Bar
MAP G4 ▪ 399 9th St at Harrison ▪ (415) 863-6623

This 1960s male-dominated bar is now popular with anybody who enjoys a fun time. Theme nights include Trannyshack, which is a fabulous drag cabaret show.

2 Make-Out Room
MAP F5 ▪ 3225 22nd St at Mission ▪ (415) 647-2888

Live music and DJ nights make this a Mission favorite. The decor is original, the drinks are cheap (try the nightly happy hour), and the staff are witty.

3 The Café
MAP E5 ▪ 2369 Market St at Castro ▪ (415) 523-0133

There is something (and somebody) for everybody at this camp, cruisy Castro old-timer that attracts home- and heterosexuals. The outdoor balcony is great for people-watching.

4 AsiaSF
MAP G4 ▪ 201 9th St at Howard ▪ (415) 255-2742

Brazen Asian drag queens are your waitresses, who also perform bar-top and stage numbers. The tropical cocktails glow in the dark. There are DJs and dancing downstairs.

5 The EndUp
MAP R4 ▪ 401 6th St at Harrison ▪ (415) 357-0827

Formerly exclusively gay, as famously featured in *Tales of the City* by Armistead Maupin *(see p45)*, this classic is now thoroughly mixed, featuring house music and an all-day Sunday "T" Dance.

6 500 Club
MAP F4 ▪ 500 Guerrero St ▪ (415) 861-2500

Cheap, stiff drinks, loud music, and plenty of seating space makes this place a trendy, local favourite. You cannot miss the neon sign that points to the entrance.

7 Slim's
MAP G4 ▪ 333 11th St ▪ (415) 255-0333

Opened by Boz Scaggs in the 1980s, Slim's has hosted touring bands from Eddie Vedder to Nirvana. The music spans roots, blues, R&B, jazz, pop, and more. Good pub food is served here.

8 El Rio
MAP F5 ▪ 3158 Mission St ▪ (415) 282-3325

Different dance events every night of the week draw a diverse crowd ready to do their thing at this bar, which opened in 1978. Sunday Salsa Showcase is particularly popular.

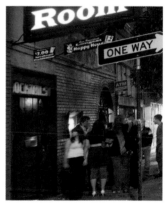

The entrance of the Elbo Room

9 Elbo Room
MAP F5 ▪ 647 Valencia St ▪ (415) 552-7788

This two-story bar combines dancing, live entertainment, and pool tables. A great mix of people come together here for the welcoming atmosphere and a great time.

10 Great Northern
MAP G4 ▪ 119 Utah St at 15th ▪ (415) 762-0151

Popular hip-hop and house DJs keep the crowds dancing at this large nightclub, which also doubles as an art gallery *(see p70)*.

See map on pp108–9

Bars

1. Café du Nord
MAP F4 ▪ 2174 Market St
▪ (415) 471-2969

Located in the landmark Swedish-American building, this subterranean restaurant and cocktail bar is one of the smartest the city has to offer.

2. Bottom of the Hill
MAP G4 ▪ 1233 17th St between Texas & Missouri ▪ (415) 626-4455

This legendary live-music venue features an assortment of punk, rock, and folk bands, plus a pleasant back patio for beer breaks *(see p70)*.

3. Nihon Whisky Lounge
MAP F4 ▪ 1779 Folsom at 14th St ▪ (415) 552-4400

The white-pebbled floor and vast selection of hard-to-find whiskys make this Japanese whisky lounge a super-cool spot to grab a drink.

Rare whisky, Nihon Whisky Lounge

4. Twenty Five Lusk
MAP H3 ▪ 25 Lusk St
▪ (415) 495-5875

Located in a renovated timber warehouse, this elegant bar-cum-restaurant is sleek and modern with a hip, urban vibe. The cocktails are delicious and the stylish lounge below is great for people-watching.

5. Bourbon & Branch
MAP P3 ▪ 501 Jones St
▪ (415) 346-1735

This classy 1920s-style speakeasy serves creative, cocktails using fresh ingredients. The secret rooms have a Prohibition-era atmosphere. Come here for hard-to-find liquors.

6. Trick Dog
MAP F5 ▪ 3010 20th St
▪ (415) 471-2999

Well-crafted and imaginative cocktails win rave reviews at

The bar at Trick Dog

this beautiful, split-level bar in the Mission District. Innovative decor and delicious bar snacks.

7. The Knockout
MAP F6 ▪ 3223 Mission St
▪ (415) 550-6994

With DJs and live music all week, and bingo on Thursdays, The Knockout has remained one of the most popular dive bars in San Francisco for years.

8. Mezzanine
MAP Q3 ▪ 444 Jesse St
▪ (415) 625-8880

This space showcases richly-diverse live and electronic music from a wide variety of genres (including rock, dance, hip-hop, soul, jazz, salsa, and world beat), as well as hosting multimedia art events and fashion shows *(see p70)*.

9. Hotel Utah Saloon
MAP R5 ▪ 500 4th St
▪ (415) 421-8308

This Gold-Rush-themed bar, with a honky-tonk atmosphere hosts live local music acts and boasts a long bar. Perch on the balcony to watch the world go by.

10. 21st Amendment
MAP R6 ▪ 563 2nd St
▪ (415) 369-0900

A sports fan's dream, this brewpub near the ballpark serves up hand-crafted beers and standard American fare. It's a friendly place to catch a game on television.

Places to Eat

PRICE CATEGORIES

For a three-course meal for one with half a bottle of wine (or equivalent meal), taxes, and extra charges.

$ under $40 $$ $40–$80 $$$ over $80

 Stable Café
MAP F5 ■ 2128 Folsom at 17th St ■ (415) 552-1199 ■ Closed D ■ $

Stable Café offers delicious homemade breakfast and lunch options that center on fresh-baked breads and healthy local ingredients.

2 Marlowe
MAP H3 ■ 500 Brannan St ■ (415) 777-1413 ■ $$

This cozy yet chic restaurant serves outstanding bistro dishes.

3 Prospect
MAP H2 ■ 300 Spear St ■ (415) 247-7770 ■ $$$

One of the city's most stand-out meals can be had at this SoMa mainstay. The decadent brunch is less pricey.

 Orphan Andy's
MAP F4 ■ 3991 17th St at Market ■ (415) 864-9795 ■ $

Open 24 hours, this friendly diner is a great spot for breakfast, often resulting in long queues.

5 Chow
MAP F4 ■ 215 Church St ■ (415) 552-2469 ■ $

Just off Market Street, Chow offers affordable pizzas, pastas, and grilled and roasted meats, as well as a selection of beers and wines. The service is friendly.

 Pancho Villa Taqueria
MAP F4 ■ 3071 16th St ■ (415) 864-8840 ■ $

This is one of the best Mexican eateries in the city, serving authentic tacos and burritos for low prices.

7 Foreign Cinema
MAP F5 ■ 2534 Mission St ■ (415) 648-7600 ■ $$

Entertaining guests by screening old and new movies as they dine, this eatery is a recurring name on the *San Francisco Chronicle*'s list of the city's top 100 restaurants *(see p74)*.

8 Caffè Centro
MAP R6 ■ 102 South Park ■ (415) 882-1500 ■ Closed Sun ■ $

Drinks, pastries, soups, and salads are served at this bustling café.

9 Osha Thai
MAP F5 ■ 819 Valencia St ■ (415) 826-7738 ■ $

A perennial favorite with the club crowd. Dishes are fresh and tasty, service is lightning fast, and prices are reasonable.

10 Delfina
MAP F5 ■ 3621 18th St ■ (415) 552-4055 ■ Closed L ■ $$

Delfina serves perfect Italian fare. Its next-door pizzeria is ideal for a more casual dinner *(see p75)*.

Interior of Italian restaurant Delfina

See map on pp108–9

🔟 Oceanfront

As with every part of the city, this area is a study in contrasts. It contains terrains of natural, untamed beauty – particularly the windswept cliffs and hidden ravines of Land's End, the scene of innumerable shipwrecks. Yet, just a few blocks away is Sea Cliff, one of the most exclusive residential neighborhoods. Of all the city's areas, this is where you're almost certain to encounter the infamous fog, but if the weather is clear there are great views of the offshore Seal Rocks and even the Farallon Islands.

Statue at Legion of Honor

OCEANFRONT

Top 10 Sights
see pp117–19

Places to Eat
see p123

Shops
see p122

0 meters 1000
0 yards 1000

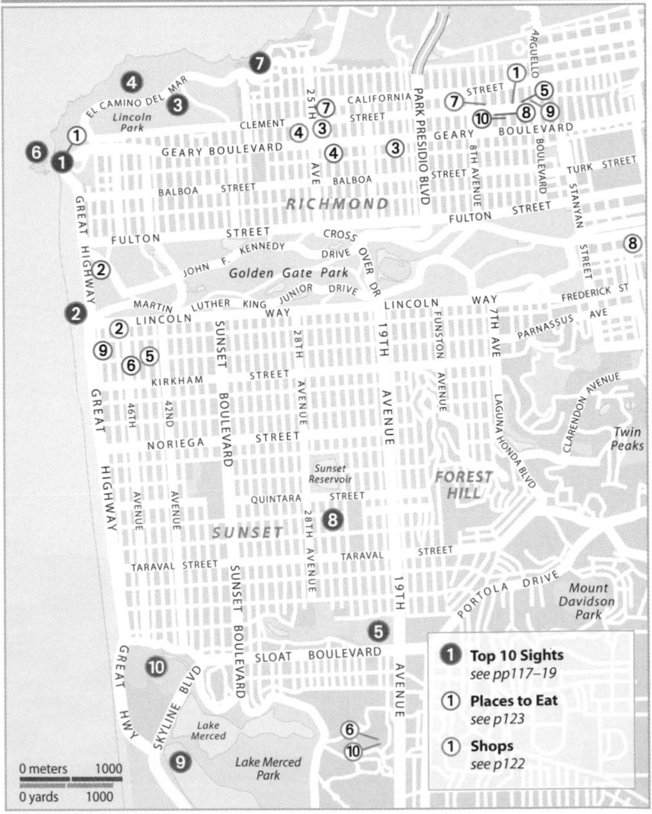

1 Cliff House
MAP A3 ■ (415) 386-3330
■ Open for lunch and dinner (call for times) ■ www.cliffhouse.com

Built in 1909, the present structure is the third on this site and was renovated in 2004. Its predecessor, a massively elaborate eight-story Victorian-Gothic castle that burned down in 1907, was built by the flamboyant entrepreneur Adolph Sutro (his estate overlooking Cliff House is now Sutro Heights Park). Cliff House has restaurants on the upper levels (see p123), observation decks overlooking the Pacific Ocean, a wing containing two bars, and the Camera Obscura, which gives a close-up view of Seal Rocks (see p118).

2 Ocean Beach
MAP A4 ■ The Great Hwy

Most of the western boundary of San Francisco is defined by this broad sweep of sand. Although it is a sublime sight when viewed from Cliff House or Sutro Heights Park, do note that the beach is dangerous to swim from due to its icy waters, rough shore breakers, and, most of all, rip currents that are powerful enough to drag even strong swimmers out to sea. Nevertheless, hardy Californian surfers in thick wetsuits are a common sight here, and in fine weather sunbathers and picnickers materialize to loll on the sand and enjoy the sunshine.

3 Legion of Honor
MAP B3 ■ Lincoln Park, 34th Ave & Clement St ■ (415) 750-3600
Open 9:30am–5:15pm Tue–Sun
■ Adm ■ www.fams.org

The creation of Alma de Bretteville Spreckels, heiress to the Spreckels sugar fortune, this museum is a replica of the Palais de la Légion d'Honneur in Paris. The original structure was built for the 1915 Panama-Pacific Exposition, but Mrs. Spreckels wanted to build a permanent version and employed the same architect she commissioned for her mansion in Pacific Heights (see p103). It opened in 1924 and features medieval to 20th-century European art, with paintings by Monet and Rembrandt. The museum also hosts excellent traveling exhibitions.

4 Oceanfront Parks
MAP A3

Lincoln Park, Lands End, and Sutro Heights Park are large green areas overlooking the coast all along this northwestern corner of the peninsula. Lincoln Park is the work of John McClaren (see p25), and features trails with some of the best views of the Golden Gate Bridge. Lands End is a rugged stretch along the cliffs that features a picturesque cove and truly spectacular hiking. Statuary of the old Sutro estate still decorates Sutro Heights Park, which dominates the coastal scene from its dramatic vantage point.

Rock labyrinth by Eduardo Aguilera at Lands End

5 Sigmund Stern Recreation Grove

Sloat Blvd at 19th Ave, Sunset ▪ (415) 252-6252 ▪ www.sterngrove.org

This 33-acre (13-ha) ravine in the southern Sunset District was donated to the city of San Francisco by Rosalie M. Stern in 1931, in memory of her husband Sigmund, a civic leader. It is the site of the nation's original free summer arts festival, Stern Grove Festival, which was endowed in 1938 and is still in operation today. Running on Sunday afternoons, the program may include classical music performed by the San Francisco Symphony Orchestra, opera, jazz, popular music, or productions by the San Francisco Ballet. The natural amphitheater, in a eucalyptus, fir, and redwood grove, has great acoustics.

6 Seal Rocks
MAP A3

The westernmost promontory on this tip of the peninsula is Point Lobos, the projection that forms the rocky cove of Land's End. Along to the south from here down to Cliff House is a scattering of small, rocky islands that are frequented by seals – hence the name. Bring binoculars with you to spy on the seals and birds in their natural habitat. At night, from the beach or Cliff House promenade, the barking of the sea lions – like the keening of the foghorns – is both reassuring and eerie, and so very "San Francisco." On a clear day, 32 miles (50 km) off the coast, you can see the Farallon Islands, which are also inhabited by sea lions and have a state-protected rookery.

Seals basking on the Seal Rocks

CLIFF HOUSE AND THE SUTRO BATHS

Adolph Sutro came to San Francisco from Prussia in 1851, aged 21 and looking for gold. He became "King of the Comstock Lode" in Nevada, and brought his riches back to the city to invest them in land. His projects included building the first Cliff House, the popular Sutro Baths, and his own lavish estate. In the process, he made the Ocean Beach area into a recreational gem. The legacy lives on, despite the disappearance of all three of the famous buildings he constructed.

---

7 Sea Cliff
MAP C2

Many famous residents, such as Twitter founder Jack Dorsey and actress Sharon Stone, have had homes in this elite residential enclave, which stands in stark contrast to the natural coastal area all around it. Most of the luxurious homes are Mediterranean in style and date from the 1920s. Just below the neighborhood, China Beach – named after poor Chinese fishermen who used to camp here – is one of the safest beaches in the city for swimming and is equipped with showers and other facilities. Baker Beach, just to the north, is another popular beach (see pp58–9).

8 Sunset District
MAP C5 ▪ Between Sloat Blvd & Golden Gate Park and Stanyan St & the Pacific Ocean

Like its counterpart, the Richmond District (see p104), this neighborhood was part of the Outer Lands and is

purely residential, consisting of row upon row of neat, lookalike houses. Yet, like the entire area along the ocean, this district is subject to a great deal of gray weather. Its one claim to fame is Sutro Tower, the pronged red-and-white television antenna that resembles something out of a science fiction movie.

9 Lake Merced
Hwy 35

Located at the beginning of scenic Skyline Boulevard (Hwy 35), this lake, set amid verdant hills, extends across the southern end of the Sunset District. Relatively undeveloped and underused, it nevertheless gets its share of recreation enthusiasts. They come for the municipal 18-hole TPC Harding Park golf course, as well as the biking and running trails that circle the lake's green shoreline.

Fishing boats on Lake Merced

10 San Francisco Zoo
Sloat Blvd at Pacific Ocean

- Buses 18 & 23 ■ (415) 753-7080
- Open 10am–4pm daily ■ Adm
- www.sfzoo.org

San Francisco Zoo is at the far southwest corner of the city, between the Pacific Ocean and Lake Merced. The complex is home to more than 1,000 species. Gorilla Preserve, Grizzly Gulch, Koala Crossing, and Children's Zoo are particular hits, as are the feeding times for the grizzly bears and the penguins. Summer brings a busy program of extra activities in the Children's Zoo.

A TWO-HOUR HIKE AROUND LAND'S END

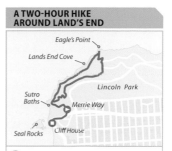

This section of the coast is amazingly wild, especially considering that it is actually within the city limits. Note that portions of the hike are very rugged, so dress accordingly, with good footwear.

Begin at the far end of the **Merrie Way** parking lot and take the steps down. Follow the trail that passes by the **Sutro Baths** ruins, to your left as you descend. Continue on along to the Overlook, from which you can take in **Seal Rocks** and much of the Pacific panorama.

Now double back a bit to pick up the trail that continues along the coast. You will see the remains of concrete military bunkers, which have been broken and tilted by the unstable land, and are now decorated with graffiti. Soon you come to a beach below rocky cliffs; note that the surging water is very unpredictable here, so be very attentive. Continue walking and you will arrive at **Land's End Cove**, where a makeshift beach, using rock walls as windbreakers, is popular with nudists.

Next, climb up one of the sets of wooden steps to join the path up above and continue on around the bend, where a stunning view of the Golden Gate Bridge *(see pp12–13)* will greet you. Continue walking all the way to **Eagle's Point** and then return by way of the higher trail that winds through **Lincoln Park** *(see p117)*.

If you have worked up an appetite from your hike, enjoy a meal and the wonderful views at **Cliff House** *(see p123)*.

See map on p116

Shops

1 Park Life
MAP D3 ■ 220 Clement St
■ (415) 386-7275

Part retail store, part art gallery, this sleek space features limited-edition books, prints, homeware, jewelry, T-shirts, and art. The gallery exhibits contemporary art.

2 The Last Straw
MAP A5 ■ 4540 Irving St
■ (415) 566-4692

This tiny store near the beach has been run by the same friendly owner for more than 30 years. Great, interesting pieces of jewelry and unique finds are on sale here.

3 Gaslight & Shadows Antiques
MAP C3 ■ 2335 Clement St
■ (415) 387-0633

The specialty here is porcelain, specifically the delicate master-pieces turned out by the various makers in the town of Limoges, France. It's like visiting a museum dedicated to this fine art form. There are dolls and costume jewelry, too.

4 Paul's Hat Works
MAP B3 ■ 6128 Geary Blvd
■ (415) 221-5332

This one-of-a-kind store is devoted to old-fashioned hat making. Each hat is custom-made.

Custom-made hats at Paul's Hat Works

5 Aqua Surf Shop
MAP A5 ■ 3847 Judah St
■ (415) 242-9283

Every sort of surf gear, including the extra-thick wetsuits needed to survive these northern waters.

6 Stonestown Galleria
3251 20th Ave at Winston Drive
■ (415) 759-2626

Upmarket Nordstrom and all-purpose Macy's are the anchor stores in this traditional indoor-outdoor shopping center with the usual array of mall stores, from Gap to Sunglass Hut, as well as plenty of food outlets.

7 Green Apple Books
MAP D3 ■ 506 Clement St
■ (415) 387-2272

It's easy to lose a few hours browsing through the selection of used books and DVDs at this store. Part of the fun is taking the time to read the well-written and helpful staff recommendations.

8 Piedmont Boutique
MAP E4 ■ 1452 Haight St
■ (415) 864-8075

A stroll around Haight-Ashbury isn't complete without a visit to Piedmont Boutique, the famous, flashy clothier to the party set for nearly a half-century.

9 Covet
MAP D3 ■ 391 Arguello St
■ (415) 751-1158

This charming shop offers vintage and vintage-inspired clothing, accessories and jewelry for women. The store has two other locations in the city.

10 See's Candies
3251 20th Ave, Stonestown Galleria ■ (415) 731-1784

Founded in 1921 by Charles See, this traditional shop offers high-quality chocolates, truffles, brittles, toffees, and lollipops.

Previous pages Golden Gate Bridge and Fort Point

Places to Eat

PRICE CATEGORIES
For a three-course meal for one with half
a bottle of wine (or equivalent meal),
taxes, and extra charges.

$ under $40 $$ $40–$80 $$$ over $80

 Cliff House
MAP A3 ▪ 1090 Point Lobos Ave
▪ (415) 386-3330 ▪ $

Standard American fare, but the
real reason to come here is to see
the Pacific crashing on the cliffs
below and to witness the wonderful
sunsets *(see p117)*.

 Beach Chalet Brewery
MAP A4 ▪ 1000 Great Hwy
▪ (415) 386-8439 ▪ $$

People come here for the
views – both of the ocean and
the murals – as well as for the food.

3 Kabuto Sushi
MAP C3 ▪ 5121 Geary Blvd at
15th Ave ▪ (415) 752-5652 ▪ Closed
Mon ▪ $$

A great Japanese restaurant – the
sashimi melts in the mouth.

4 Ton Kiang
MAP C3 ▪ 5821 Geary Blvd
▪ (415) 387-8273 ▪ $

Many say this restaurant has the
best dim sum on offer in the city.
Always fresh, hot, and tasty, with
various specialties.

5 Chapeau!
MAP C3 ▪ 126 Clement St at
2nd Ave ▪ (415) 387-0408 ▪ Closed L
▪ $$$

A memorably authentic French
bistro. The sommelier can direct
you to fine wines that pair well
with the classic fare, which
includes *filet mignon*.

6 Outerlands
MAP A3 ▪ 4001 Judah St
▪ (415) 661-6140 ▪ $

Grab a table outside, or enjoy the rustic
interior, here. Feast on the creative,

Brunch dishes at Outerlands

organic-based menus, offering fresh
seafood, veggie soups and sand-
wiches, and exotic salads. They
serve great cocktails, too. Come
early for the popular Sunday brunch.

7 Pizzetta 211
MAP C3 ▪ 211 23rd Ave
▪ (415) 379-9880 ▪ $

Thin and crisp pizza topped with
organic ingredients from fragrant
aioli to home-made sausage.

8 Café Bunn Mi
MAP D3 ▪ 417 Clement St
▪ (415) 668-8908 ▪ $

Vietnamese sandwiches at their
best, and for a bargain, too.

9 Java Beach Café
MAP A5 ▪ 1396 La Playa St
▪ (415) 665-5282 ▪ $

This cozy café serves sandwiches,
soup, and pastries in a nautical-
themed interior.

10 Burma Superstar
MAP D3 ▪ 309 Clement St
▪ (415) 387-2147 ▪ $

This Burmese eatery boasts
an extensive menu of flavorsome
noodles, curries, and salads.

See map on p116

TOP 10 The Bay Area

In local parlance, the Bay Area includes the City, the East Bay, Marin, the Peninsula, and the South Bay. Although Santa Clara, San Jose, Santa Cruz, and Capitola do not touch the waters of the Bay, they embody the same open-minded ethos that defines it. This is probably because the mentality of this swatch of Northern California is so different from that of Southern California. In towns like Berkeley the emphasis is on progressive thinking, whilst smaller enclaves like Bolinas live life in harmony with the breathtaking nature all around them.

Oakland's Paramount Theatre

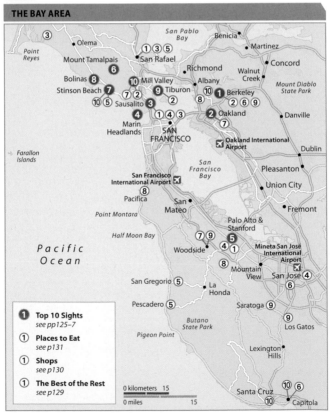

THE BAY AREA

Top 10 Sights
see pp125–7

Places to Eat
see p131

Shops
see p130

The Best of the Rest
see p129

0 kilometers   15
0 miles   15

Houseboats in the former fishing community of Sausalito

① Berkeley
BART Downtown Berkeley

Known as "Berzerkeley," for the student dissent of the 1960s, today the tree-shaded UC Berkeley campus is still the center of TV-worthy protests. At one of the world's greatest universities, "Cal's" faculty boasts many Nobel laureates. This diversity-proud East Bay city is abundant with gourmet cafés and ethnic restaurants. Fourth street is sprinkled with shops, while the parks, as well as the biking and hiking trails appeal to those wishing to escape the bustle of city life.

② Oakland
BART 12th St

Notorious for racial unrest and crime in the past, Oakland is now a multicultural haven for artists, musicians, and those fleeing the high rents of San Francisco. The city's attractions include the huge Lake Merritt, which offers a range of recreational possibilities, the Museum of California *(see p128)*, the Oakland Zoo, two glorious Art Deco-era theaters (Paramount and Fox), the Jack London Square waterfront complex of eateries and shops, the USS Potomac (FDR's Floating White House), and a ferry landing. In the hills, you will find a beautiful Mormon Temple, with dazzling Bay views, the sprawling Redwood Regional Park, and the Chabot Space and Science Center.

③ Sausalito
US 101

A former fishing community and now an upscale commuter area and tourist haven, this small town offers spectacular views of San Francisco from its Bridgeway Avenue promenade. Historically, it has been an artists' town, home to an eccentric mix of residents. Bungalows cling to the hillsides and boats fill the picturesque marinas, many of them are houseboats that locals live in year-round. There are excellent restaurants, places to stay, and some unique shopping possibilities, too.

④ Marin Headlands
Muni Bus 76

To visit these raw, wild hills with astonishingly beautiful views is to enter another world; yet it's only half an hour's drive from the city, via the Golden Gate Bridge. The scale of the rolling terrain is immense, and the precipitous drops into the ocean are dramatic. This is an unspoiled area of wildlife (Point Reyes to the north is home to tule elk herds), windswept ridges, sheltered valleys, and deserted beaches *(see p58)*.

Tule elk, Point Reyes

Stanford University, Palo Alto

⑤ Palo Alto and Stanford
Hwys 101 & 82

An erstwhile sleepy university town, Palo Alto has experienced a boom as the focal point of Silicon Valley, and driving force of the "New Economy." Although a lot of the gilding has lately fallen off the lily, this town has been left with a considerably dressed-up appearance, as well as many fancy restaurants, hotels, and shops. The town is home to prestigious private Stanford University, with its beautiful, well-tended campus (see p65).

GREAT BAY AREA UNIVERSITIES

Palo Alto's Stanford University is the Bay Area's most famous private institution of higher learning, inaugurated in 1891. However, in terms of intellectual clout, the University of California at Berkeley, the oldest campus in the California system, stands shoulder to shoulder, considering the number of Nobel laureates on the faculty and its international importance. Stanford is known for business, law, and medicine, whilst Berkeley is famed for law, engineering, and nuclear physics. Both universities are among the most selective in the entire country.

---

⑥ Mount Tamalpais
Hwy 1

From the summit of 2,570-ft (785-m) "Mount Tam," sacred to the Native Americans who once lived here, practically the entire Bay Area can be seen. The area is a state park, with more than 200 miles (320 km) of trails through redwood groves and alongside creeks. There are picnic areas, campsites, an open-air theater, and meadows for kite flying.

Mountain Theatre, Mount Tamalpais

⑦ Stinson Beach
Hwy 1

Since the early 20th century, this has been a popular vacation spot and remains the preferred swimming beach for the whole area (see p58). The soft sand and the spectacular sunsets set off the quaint village, with its good restaurants and interesting shops. You can reach it via the coast route, but the drive up Highway 1 gives the most dramatic arrival, with inspiring views as you exit the forest onto the headlands.

8 Bolinas
Hwy 1

Bolinas is a hippie village that time forgot. The citizens regularly take down road signs showing the way to their special place, to keep away visitors. Potters and other craftspeople sell their wares in the funky gallery, organic produce and vegetarianism are the rule, and 1960s idealism still predominates.

"Ark Row" shops, Tiburon

9 Tiburon
Hwy 131

Marin County's less hectic alternative to Sausalito – here, 100-year-old houseboats ("arks") have been pulled ashore and refurbished, forming "Ark Row." It houses shops, restaurants, and cafés that enhance the charm of this waterfront village. There are also opportunities to see wildlife in the parks along the shore, facing Angel Island and the city.

10 Mill Valley
Off Hwy 101

Home to a well-known film festival, this is the quintessential Marin town; wealthy, relaxed, beautiful, and with a well-educated populace given to liberal views on just about every topic. The old part of town is flanked by redwoods, lined with old buildings housing restaurants and unusual shops, and the whole centers around an eternally pleasant public square.

A MORNING WALK AROUND BERKELEY

Begin at the **UC Berkeley Visitor Center** at 101 Sproul Hall near the intersection of Bancroft Way and Telegraph Avenue, where you can pick up information and maps. Follow around to University Drive and on to the university campus, passing Romanesque **Wellman Hall**, then take a left on Cross Campus Road. Straight ahead is the main campus landmark, the 307-ft (94-m) **Sather Tower**, also known simply as the Campanile, based on the famous bell tower in Venice's Piazza San Marco.

Now continue on to rejoin University Drive and go around to the **Hearst Greek Theatre**, venue for excellent concerts of all sorts. Next, head for handsome Sather Gate, which leads into **Sproul Plaza**, epicenter of the student Free Speech Movement protests that erupted into almost nonstop sociopolitical unrest in the 1960s and 1970s.

Exit the campus onto Telegraph Avenue, a kind of East Bay Haight-Ashbury with radical vibes all its own, and once home of the legendary bookstore Cody's, controversially closed in 2008. One block over is idealistic **People's Park**. Continue on back to Bancroft Way to pay a visit to the **Berkeley Art Museum** and the **Pacific Film Archive**.

After your walk, head over to **The Cheese Board Collective** (1512 Shattuck Ave at Vine St; (510) 549-3183). The restaurant serves homemade vegetarian pizzas with creative toppings such as asparagus, Gouda, and gremolata.

See map on p124

Oakland Museum of California

1 **The Building**
The museum building is an outstanding example of modern design. Opened in 1969, it is composed of reinforced concrete and consists of three levels of tiered terraces. To soften the angularity, roof gardens have been planted, accented with sculpture.

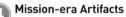
Oakland Museum of California

2 **Natural Sciences**
In the brilliant Gallery of California Natural Sciences, the state is presented as one of the world's top ten biological "hot spots." There are thousands of artifacts on display, including bird and mammal study skins and mounts, as well as an enormous collection of reptiles, amphibians, and fungi.

3 **Gold Rush Artifacts**
The lives of those who came to California from all over the world in the 19th century, hoping to strike it rich, are chronicled here. You'll see gold nuggets, prospecting tools and rare mining equipment.

Gold nugget

4 **Mission-era Artifacts**
A 19th-century icon of St. Peter is just one remnant of the Spanish Mission years you'll find here, where there are also colonial tools, and part of a Spanish ship.

5 **The Earliest Californians**
Fascinating galleries explore early human history in the state of California, documented by materials such as basketry, stone tools, clothing, and objects used in rituals.

6 **Earthquake Artifacts**
A collection of objects that pertain to the terrible earthquake of 1906 are on display here, including porcelain cups and saucers fused together by the heat of the fire that destroyed so much of the city.

7 **Californian History**
This section of the museum has exhibits associated with technology, agriculture, business, and domestic life from the early Native Americans up to the 21st century. Subjects such as World War II, baby boomers, Hollywood, and Silicon Valley are also covered.

8 **Art Gallery**
The third level of the museum is devoted to the Gallery of California Art, featuring works by artists who have studied, lived, and worked here. Included are works by California Impressionists and members of the Bay Area Figurative Movement. Check the website (www.museumca.org) for the opening times of the California Art and History Galleries.

9 **Photography**
The Gallery of California Art also has an impressive collection of the work of California photographers, including Ansel Adams, Edward Weston, and Dorothea Lange.

10 **Californian Crafts**
This is the largest collection in the world of work by California Arts and Crafts practitioners Arthur and Lucia Kleinhans Mathews, including paintings, drawings, furniture, and other decorative art.

The Best of the Rest

① San Rafael
Hwy 101

This town has a charming historic center with good restaurants and shops. A street market transforms the main drag into a bustling hub every Thursday evening.

② Belvedere Island

This garden island, attached by a causeway to Tiburon, is one of the Bay's most exclusive residential areas. Worth a visit to see the palatial homes and their sumptuous setting.

③ Point Reyes
Hwy 1 to Olema, then signposted to Point Reyes

This windswept peninsula is a haven for wildlife, including a herd of tule elk; it is also home to cattle ranches. You can watch migrating whales offshore from December to March.

④ San Jose
Hwy 101

This sprawling town is an integral part of Silicon Valley enterprises and has popular attractions.

⑤ San Gregorio and Pescadero
Hwy 1

Sheltered by cliffs, San Gregorio is the Bay Area's oldest nude beach. It is adjacent to the Pescadero State Beach, which has lots of tide pools. The fishing village evokes the Old West, complete with a white-washed wooden church. Duarte's Tavern has been serving artichoke soup and olallieberry pie since 1894.

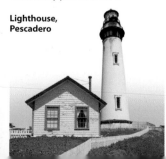
Lighthouse, Pescadero

⑥ Winchester Mystery House
525 S Winchester Blvd, San Jose ▪ (408) 247-2101 ▪ **Open daily (call for tour times)** ▪ **Adm**

The eccentric 19th-century home of the rifle heiress, Sarah Winchester, took 38 years to build and includes stairways leading to nowhere and windows set into floors.

Winchester Mystery House

⑦ Woodside
Hwy 280

This bucolic residential area is where many of the first families to have lived in the Bay Area built fabulous mansions in the late 19th century.

⑧ Pacifica
Hwy 1 off Hwy 280

A popular weekend destination, this oceanfront city is great for surfing, fishing, cycling, golf, and hiking. Lodgings and seafood restaurants face the ocean and the quaint little downtown is lined with shops.

⑨ Los Gatos and Saratoga
Hwy 280

These tree-lined small towns, full of restaurants and shops, have become upscale communities for the movers and shakers of Silicon Valley.

⑩ Santa Cruz and Capitola
Hwy 1

Some of the Central Coast's best swimming, plus the Boardwalk, a famous vintage amusement park.

See map on p124

Shops

1 Stanford Shopping Center

660 Stanford Shopping Center, Palo Alto ■ Hwy 101 ■ (650) 617-8200

One of the first shopping centers in the Bay Area, this outdoor mall is dog-friendly and features shops that you don't tend to find everywhere, such as Kate Spade, Free People, and Bloomingdales.

2 Powell's Sweet Shoppe
3206 College Ave, Berkeley ■ Hwy 80 ■ (510) 658-9866

This old-fashioned candy store features row upon row of brightly colored gummy candies, chocolates, and lollipops, plus a number of vintage penny candies and novelty confectionery, such as bacon soda.

Candy at Powell's Sweet Shoppe

3 Gene Hiller
729 Bridgeway Ave, Sausalito ■ Hwy 101 ■ (415) 332-3636

Since 1953, this menswear store has been offering the finest imported designer clothing – from classic formal to casual – including Ermenegildo Zegna and Canali.

4 Shady Lane

325 Sharon Park Drive, Menlo Park ■ Off Hwy 280 ■ (650) 321-1099

This boutique was founded by a collective of artists who wanted to create a showcase for their designs in areas like jewelry and ceramics.

5 Via Diva

516 Irwin St, San Rafael ■ Off Hwy 101 ■ (415) 257-8881

This broad collection of art and artifacts includes treasures from China, Indonesia, India, Thailand, and South America.

6 Treehouse Green Gifts
2935 College Ave, Berkeley ■ Hwy 80 ■ (510) 204-9292

This eco-friendly store sells home accessories, garden items, and gifts for babies and kids, all produced by unique artists.

7 Margaret O'Leary
14 Miller Ave, Mill Valley ■ Off Hwy 101 ■ (415) 388-2390

Mill Valley is home to the flagship store of this acclaimed women's knitwear label, known for its classic, upscale takes on California comfort.

8 Convert
1809B 4th St, Berkeley ■ Hwy 101 ■ (510) 649-9759

This trendy boutique, selling clothes and shoes for men and women, focuses on sustainably sourced lines.

9 Fourth Street
Berkeley ■ (510) 644-3002

A tree-shaded warren of boutiques and galleries, this popular street in Berkeley is lined by the likes of The Gardener, Sur La Table, Stained Glass Garden, Builders Booksource, and Jeffrey's Toys.

10 Claudia Chapline Gallery and Sculpture Garden
3445 Shoreline Hwy, Stinson Beach ■ Hwy 1 ■ (415) 868-2308

In a great setting near the beach, the Chapline sculpture garden is full of delights, especially Lyman Whitaker's brilliant kinetic pieces, which are driven by the wind. Inside, the variety and quality of painted and mixed-media work is very compelling.

Shady Lane at Sharon Park Drive

Places to Eat

PRICE CATEGORIES
For a three-course meal for one with half a bottle of wine (or equivalent meal), taxes, and extra charges.

$ under $40 $$ $40–$80 $$$ over $80

① Poggio Trattoria
777 Bridgeway, Sausalito
(415) 332-7771 $$

Overlooking the waterfront, this classic, upscale trattoria serves award-winning Northern Italian food alongside. There is also a list of fabulous cocktails on offer. Grab a booth or a sidewalk table.

② Vasco
106 Throckmorton Ave, Mill Valley Hwy 101 & Hwy 1 (415) 381-3343 Closed L $

Vasco serves delicious pizzas, pastas, and desserts. The downside is there's often a wait for a table.

③ Sol Food
901 Lincoln Ave, San Rafael Hwy 101 (415) 451-4765 $

Locals and tourists alike line up for a taste of the flavorful, festive Puerto Rican food at this bright restaurant. There is a special dish on the menu, which changes every day.

④ The Bridgeway Café
633 Bridgeway, Sausalito Hwy 101 (415) 332-3426 $

You'll find a range of American favorites at this cozy little diner looking onto the Bay.

⑤ Parkside Snack Bar
43 Arenal Ave, Stinson Beach Hwy 1 (415) 868-1272 $

Creative brunch at picnic tables on the patio, or in the dining room. Try the Tomales Bay mussels.

⑥ Gayle's
504 Bay Ave, Capitola Hwy 1 (831) 462-1200 $

This bakery and *rosticceria* (or deli) features an extraordinary selection

A selection of cakes at Gayle's

of gourmet treats, both sweet and savory. Try the Opera Cake and the to-die-for cupcakes.

⑦ Café Eritrea d'Afrique
4069 Telegraph Ave, Oakland Hwy 880 (510) 547-4520 $

An acclaimed restaurant serving Eritrean and Ethiopian cuisine in a relaxing and friendly atmosphere. They offer an all-you-can-eat veggie buffet on Wednesdays and Fridays.

⑧ Alpine Inn
3915 Alpine Rd, Portola Valley Hwy 280 (650) 854-4004 $

In a building that dates back to 1850, this greasy beer bar with a garden is popular with locals and Silicon Valley workers alike for its substantial burgers and fries.

⑨ Buck's
3062 Woodside Drive, Woodside Hwy 280 (650) 851-8010 $

After a long hike on one of the many trails in Woodside, enjoy a hearty Woodsider omelet and coffee at this kitsch restaurant.

⑩ Chez Panisse
1517 Shattuck Ave, Berkeley Hwy 80 (510) 548-5525 Closed Sun $$$

A popular Berkeley spot which has been serving up excellent California cuisine, using organic seasonal ingredients, since 1971. The upstairs café offers a cheaper alternative.

See map on p124

Streetsmart

**The crooked turns of
Lombard Street**

Getting To and Around San Francisco

Arriving by Air

Three international airports serve the San Francisco Bay Area, all linked by public transportation to one another.

San Francisco International Airport (SFO) is 14 miles (23 km) south of the city. It is one of the busiest airports on Earth, with over 40 airlines from around the world operating here. However, it is also one of the most user-friendly.

The airport's **Bay Area Rapid Transit** (BART) station is connected to the terminals by a light-rail shuttle (although it stops frequently, so allow time for the journey). BART connects to four Downtown stations, and to **Caltrain**, which connects to San Jose.

Rental cars, taxis, limousines, and shuttles to surrounding cities and Downtown hotels are available at the airport. There are some minibus companies, such as **BayPorter Express** and **American Airporter Shuttle**, that offer a door-to-door shuttle service, taking passengers to a specific address. The cost of the trip is shared with the other passengers. A taxi ride from SFO into the city averages at about $50 plus tip.

Oakland International Airport (OAK) is a half-hour **AC Transit** bus ride across the Bay from San Francisco. There is good transportation into San Francisco by door-to-door bus, car, and limousine shuttle services. The airport is served by BART and connects to four San Francisco stations.

Mineta San Jose International Airport (SJC), in the heart of Silicon Valley, is 45 miles (72 km) south of San Francisco. **SamTrans** provides a 24-hour bus service to the city and San Mateo County. BART and Caltrain also provide transport from SJC into San Francisco.

Arriving by Bus

Greyhound buses arrive in the city from across the country to the station at 200 Folsom Street. The most affordable but time-consuming way to cover long distances in the US, buses usually have power outlets and free Wi-Fi.

Arriving by Train

Amtrak trains access San Francisco from stations across the country. The closest station is Emeryville, to the north of Oakland. Amtrak runs a free shuttle to the city center.

Arriving by Sea

Cruise ships dock at Pier 27, which is the embarkation and debarkation point of many Alaskan or Mexican Riviera cruises. Taxis and modes of public transportation are available at the dock.

Traveling by Bus, Muni Metro, and Cable Car

The San Francisco Municipal Railway, or **Muni** as it is commonly called, runs the city buses, Muni Metro light rail, cable cars, and streetcars. Purchase money- and time-saving Muni passports, which can be used on all the above modes of transport.

As much tourist attraction as transportation, **cable cars** and vintage streetcars trundle in style around city streets. The world-famous cable cars run between Market Street and Fisherman's Wharf, on the north–south Powell-Mason and Powell-Hyde lines, and on the east–west California Street line.

Bay Area Rapid Transit (BART)

BART operates 6 fast routes to 46 stations throughout the city. Trains run from 4am to midnight, every 15 minutes during the week. On Saturdays, they run from 6am, and on Sundays from 8am, every 20 minutes. Trains sometimes run after midnight for special events.

Transport Passes

The **Clipper** card gives passengers access to all participating Bay Area transport, including Muni (except cable cars) and BART, with an easy-to-use, reloadable card that does not expire. Purchase them at Muni vending machines in subway stations and at many retailers. Muni tickets can also be purchased for single or round-trip rides, and reloaded as needed. Just tap the card or ticket at the Clipper reader upon entering a faregate or boarding a vehicle. **CityPass** saves up to 42 per cent on unlimited cable car and Muni rides, plus admission to four city attractions.

By Taxi and Ride Services

Taxis are easy to get at the airport, but often hard to catch in the city, even when you call for them; the best chance is to order one from a major Downtown hotel. **Uber** and **Lyft** are popular ride services that pick

passengers up efficiently wherever they are in the city. You order your ride and pay for it by cell phone.

By Car

Many visitors leave their cars at their lodgings, as expensive parking garages, sparse street parking, and congestion can make driving frustrating and time-consuming, even in this small, compact city. Reliable car rental agencies include **Hertz**, **SFO Rental Car Center**, and **Zipcar**.

By Bicycle

In this bicycle-friendly city, there are miles of designated lanes and parking spaces, as well as easy bicycle transport options on public transportation. SFO has a

station where riders can disassemble or assemble their bicycles, and boxes available for checking bicycles in as luggage (see **SFO Bike Information**). For cycling routes and further information, see **SF Bicycle Coalition**.

By Ferry

A breezy way to get around the Bay Area is by the many passenger ferries that arrive at Fisherman's Wharf and the Ferry Building from Marin County and the East Bay, such as **Golden Gate Ferry** and **San Francisco Bay Ferry**. From the Ferry Building at the foot of Market Street, myriad public transportation is available. **Blue and Gold Fleet** offers exciting Bay cruises.

DIRECTORY

ARRIVING BY AIR

AC Transit
w actransit.org

American Airporter Shuttle
w americanairporter.com

Bay Area Rapid Transit
w bart.gov

BayPorter Express
w bayporter.com

Caltrain
w caltrain.com

Mineta San Jose International Airport
w flysanjose.com

Oakland International Airport
w oaklandairport.com

SamTrans
w samtrans.com

San Francisco International Airport
w flysfo.com

ARRIVING BY BUS

Greyhound
w greyhound.com

ARRIVING BY TRAIN

Amtrak
w amtrak.com

TRAVELING BY BUS, MUNI METRO AND CABLE CAR

Cable Cars
w sfcablecar.com

Muni
w sfmta.com

TRANSPORT PASSES

CityPass
w citypass.com

Clipper
w clippercard.com

BY TAXI AND RIDE SERVICES

Lyft
w lyft.com

Uber
w uber.com

BY CAR

Hertz
w hertz.com

SFO Rental Car Center
w flysfo.com

Zipcar
w zipcar.com

BY BICYCLE

SF Bicycle Coalition
w sfbike.org

SFO Bike Information
w flysfo.com/to-from/biking

BY FERRY

Blue and Gold Fleet
w blueandgoldfleet.com

Golden Gate Ferry
w goldengateferry.org

San Francisco Bay Ferry
w sanfranciscobayferry.com

Practical Information

Passports and Visas

All travelers to the US need a valid passport. Most European citizens, as well as citizens from Australia, New Zealand, and Japan, need a non-refundable return ticket from outside the US to qualify for the Visa Waiver Program (VWP), which allows citizens of par-ticipating countries to enter the US without a visa for stays of 90 days or less. The **Electronic System for Travel Authorization** is an automated system that determines visitors' eligibility for the VWP.

Other nationalities must secure a visa from a US consulate or embassy before travel-ing. All major countries have **consulates** in San Francisco; for questions about visiting, contact your national representative.

Customs Regulations

You are allowed to bring in 1.75 pints (1 liter) of wine or liquor, 200 cigarettes, 100 cigars, 3 lb (1.3 kg) of tobacco, and $100 worth of gifts. Some items are not allowed, such as certain fruits and vegetables, animals, and animal products. You may carry up to $10,000 in US or foreign currency out of or into the country; larger sums must be declared, which entails filing form CM 4790. See the **US Customs and Border Protection** website for details.

Travel Safety Advice

Visitors can get up-to-date travel safety information from the Foreign and Commonwealth Office (FCO) in the **UK**, the State Department in the **US**, and the Department of Foreign Affairs and Trade in **Australia**.

Travel Insurance

Travel insurance is invaluable when you need to cancel a trip because of illness, death of a relative, weather, or emergency medical care and evacu-ation, as well as to cover lost baggage or canceled flights. **Insure My Trip** sells travel coverage from several carriers; you enter your trip details and your needs in order to receive several quotes. **Europ Assistance USA** offers multilingual, 24-hour assistance including medical evacuation, emergency cash, help with lost documents and baggage, and medical case management.

Health

No vaccinations are required for visitors to the US. San Francisco's major hospitals include **Saint Francis Memorial Hospital, Davies Medical Center**, and **Zuckerberg San Francisco General Hospital**. For minor medi-cal issues, walk-in clinics are found throughout the city, including **Care Practice** and **Traveler Medical Group**. Often you will be asked to arrange for payment before the treatment. Confirm in advance that the hospital or clinic accepts your insurance coverage. Pharmacies are located within most large chain supermarkets.

The drop-in **San Francisco City Clinic** provides free or low-cost diagnosis and treatment of STDs, plus free condoms, emergency contraception, and post-exposure prevention.

Personal Security

Dial 911 for the **emergency services**, and have your information and location ready. As in all cities, when parking, you should remove or stash valuables out of sight and lock your car. Patronize parking garages that have attendants on duty. Take care with your belongings while sitting at sidewalk tables and in crowds. Be alert after dark in the Lower Haight, the Mission, Golden Gate Park, Fisherman's Wharf, and in the Tenderloin. For personal items lost on Muni, contact **Muni Lost and Found**. For contact details of the **SFO Lost and Found**, see the airport's website.

Tourist Information

The **San Francisco Visitor Information Center** is loaded with information, coupons, tour tickets, and money-saving passes for visitors. Well in advance of your arrival, check out the website with its "trip ideas" and "deals" sections, and calendar of events. You can also use it to book hotels and request a free Visitor's Guide by mail or download a digital version. At the center itself, you can pick up CityPasses, Muni passports, and maps, and make use of the Wi-Fi and computers for free.

Gay and Lesbian Travelers

One of the most gay-friendly cities in the world, San Francisco offers plenty of LGBT-welcoming hotels and nightspots, particularly in the lively Castro district where many gay residents live. The organizer of the largest annual event in the city, the San Francisco Pride parade,

San Francisco Pride publishes an online calendar of events of interest to LGBT visitors. The **LGBT Center** is also a great source of information.

Travelers with Specific Needs

Disabled access is extensive throughout the city, from ramped curbs to telecommunication devices for hearing-impaired travelers. Discounted fares for disabled passengers are available on all transit. The free **Muni Access Guide** is available on the Muni website, and gives pointers on how to make the most of the system. Some Muni

buses hydraulically assist wheelchair-bound people to board and be secured.

Access Northern California provides information on accessible travel and recreation throughout the region. National parks offer free admission for disabled and fellow passengers In the same vehicle, and many city attractions offer reduced entrance fees. The San Francisco Visitor Information Center publishes the free Access San Francisco Guide.

Parking spaces reserved for the disabled are marked by a blue-and-white sign and a blue curb.

Accessible toilets for the disabled are provided in many places, including hotels and public buildings.

DIRECTORY

PASSPORTS AND VISAS

Australian Consulate General
MAP P5 ■ 576 Market St
[(415) 644-3620

British Consulate General
MAP P5 ■ 1 Sansome St
[(415) 617-1300

Canadian Consulate General
MAP N5 ■ 580 California St
[(415) 834-3180

Electronic System for Travel Authorization
w esta.cbp.dhs.gov

CUSTOMS

US Customs and Border Protection
w cbp.gov

TRAVEL SAFETY ADVICE

Australia
w dfat.gov.au
w smartraveller.gov.au

UK
w gov.uk/foreign-travel-advice

US
w travel.state.gov

TRAVEL INSURANCE

Europ Assistance USA
w europassistance-usa.com

Insure My Trip
w insuremytrip.com

HEALTH SERVICES

Care Practice
MAP F4 ■ 508A 14th St
[(415) 864-4444

Davies Medical Center
MAP E4 ■ 45 Castro St
[(415) 600-6000

Saint Francis Memorial Hospital
MAP N2 ■ 900 Hyde St
[(415) 353-6300

San Francisco City Clinic
MAP G4 ■ 356 7th St
[(415) 487-5500

Traveler Medical Group
MAP P3 ■ 490 Post St
[(415) 963-4398

Zuckerberg San Francisco General Hospital
MAP G5 ■ 1001 Potrero Ave
[(415) 206-8000

PERSONAL SECURITY

Emergency Services
[911

Muni Lost and Found
[311 or (415) 701 2311

SFO Lost and Found
w flysfo.com

TOURIST INFORMATION

San Francisco Visitor Information Center
MAP Q3 ■ 900 Market St
w sftravel.com

GAY AND LESBIAN TRAVELERS

LGBT Center
w sfcenter.org

San Francisco Pride
w sfpride.org

TRAVELERS WITH SPECIFIC NEEDS

Access Northern California
w accessnca.org

Muni Access Guide
w sfmta.com

Currency and Banking

US bank notes come in denominations of $1, $5, $10, $20, $50, and $100. Coins are 1c, 5c (nickel), 10c (dime), 25c (quarter), and the less common 50c and $1. Currency exchange is available at the three international airports, at Downtown banks and hotels, and at **Currency Exchange International**.

ATMs are the best way to get cash. To avoid the fees added to ATM transactions, make a purchase in a store and ask for cash. Debit cards are accepted for every transaction type.

Without a credit card, you will not be able to rent a car or check into a hotel. Visa and MasterCard are accepted everywhere, while Discover and Diners Club cards are often refused, and even American Express may be refused at smaller businesses.

Travelers' checks are no longer widely accepted, even sometimes by the banks that issue them.

Postal Services

Most US post offices are open from 9am to 5:30pm Monday to Friday and from 9am to 2pm on Saturdays. The **Union Square Post Office** is centrally located. Stamps are also available at some hotels, chain supermarkets and drugstores.

Telephone and Internet

San Francisco's area codes are 415 and 628. Surrounding cities have other area codes: you dial 1 followed by the area code. Toll-free numbers start with 800, 877, 888, or similar prefixes. Dial 411 to get local and national numbers. International calls should be preceded by 011. To save money, buy a phone card or a cheap cellphone. Cellphones can also be rented from **InTouch USA**.

Wi-Fi is free at the airports and at cafés and lodgings. You can also access free Wi-Fi in public spaces by connecting to #SFWiFi. Find more hot spots at the **Open WiFi Spots** website. Computers are available to use for free at the San Francisco Visitor Information Center and libraries.

Newspapers, Magazines, TV, and Radio

Besides publishing a daily newspaper, the **San Francisco Chronicle** maintains a website of news, events, performing arts, restaurant and movie reviews, and travel tips and articles. Lighthearted, liberal, and free, **SF Weekly** covers the arts, events, and eateries, in print and online. Both free, the **Bay Area Reporter** and **San Francisco Bay Times** cater to the LGBT community. **San Francisco Magazine** (print and online) and **7x7** (only online) are urban-lifestyle publications covering topics such as fashion, entertainment, culture, and food in the Bay Area.

The Bay Area hosts every major TV and radio network. For local news, traffic, and weather, tune into **KGO** TV and radio.

Opening Hours

Shops are generally open daily from 10am to 5pm or later. Some groceries, drugstores, and supermarkets are open daily from 7am to 11pm. Chain stores and malls are often open on holidays.

Banks are open from 9am to 5pm Monday to Friday, some are open on weekends. Museums and attractions have their own hours; most are open daily.

Time Difference

Contiguous US is divided into four time zones, with San Francisco in the Pacific Time Zone. It's 3 hours behind New York and 8 hours behind London. Daylight Saving Time moves the clock one hour ahead from the second Sunday in March until the first Sunday in November.

Electrical Appliances

The US uses 110–120 volts AC. If your appliances use 220–240 volts (as in most of Europe), bring a 110-volt transformer and a plug adapter with two flat parallel pins.

Driving

Foreign drivers' licenses are recognized in the US. Take care to notice parking signs; parking tickets are expensive and towing fees run into hundreds of dollars. When you park in this hilly city pointing uphill, turn your wheels toward the center of the street; when pointing downhill, turn your wheels toward the sidewalk. After coming to a complete stop, you can turn right at a red light after yielding to traffic and pedestrians. Watch carefully for the ubiquitous one-way streets.

All passengers must wear seat belts. Infants under 2 years must be in the backseat in a rear-facing car seat until they reach 40 lb (18.4 kg). Children under 8 must be secured in a car seat or booster seat in the backseat. Those 4 ft 9 inches (1.5 m) or taller may be secured by a safety belt in the backseat. If your child does not have a car seat, you may be denied boarding a van or taxi, or stopped by police while driving and fined $100–$250. For rental cars, reserve your car seat(s) when booking the vehicle.

Weather

The Pacific marine climate means mild year-round weather, with temperatures seldom rising above 70° F (21° C) or falling below 40° F (5° C). Bring layers – evenings are nearly always cool, and fog can roll in any day, especially in the summer time.

Natural Disasters

As major fault lines are found throughout the San Francisco Bay Area, earthquakes do occur from time to time. The biggest danger is from things falling, so if you are inside, do not run outside where there are street signs, traffic lights, power lines, and trees. Stay calm and move away from windows and mirrors. If you are in bed, lie on the floor next to the mattress. In a minute or so, the tremors should stop. Smaller aftershocks may ensue. Californians know that to be ready for any natural disaster, they should have enough supplies to last 72 hours.

Shopping

One of the most expensive shopping cities in the world, San Francisco also has plenty of ethnic neighborhoods where bargains and souvenirs can be had. High-end department stores and designer boutiques cluster around Union Square, while antiques shops and fine art galleries line up at Jackson Square. Union and Chestnut Streets are window-shoppers' meccas. There are vintage, boutique, and ethnic stores, galleries, and crafts emporiums to be discovered on Fillmore and Haight Streets and in Hayes Valley. In the Mission District, both funky fashion and Latino-style decor and apparel can be found. Chinatown and Japantown attract tourists after Asian trinkets and souvenirs.

The massive, upscale Westfield San Francisco Center is on Market Street (see p79) and Crocker Galleria lures fashionistas and Downtown office workers. Embarcadero Center on the waterfront is a four-block-square, high-rise complex of more than 100 shops and restaurants (see p79).

At Fisherman's Wharf, indoor/outdoor malls cater to visitors with restaurants, live entertainment, and boutique and souvenir stores. Other malls include Ghirardelli Square (see p79), The Cannery (see p17), Anchorage Square Shopping Center (see p16), and Pier 39 (see p16).

Dining

San Francisco has more restaurants per capita than any other US city and chefs are celebrities in this town of foodies. Reflecting the city's cultural diversity, eateries run the gamut from Mexican *taquerías* to Italian pasta houses, from Chinatown's dim sum parlors to sushi bars in Japantown, and from all-American diners to some of the best French restaurants outside Europe. The Bay Area was the birthplace of California Cuisine, an approach to fresh, seasonal, local ingredients, and dramatic presentation that changed American restaurant fare forever. Many of the trendy restaurants in the city are melding California Cuisine with the exotic tastes of Southeast Asia, China, and Japan, a combination called Asian Fusion. Locals love their neighborhood Thai, Indian, Chinese, and Italian restaurants where they can fill up without having to empty their wallets.

Pacific Ocean seafood tops the menus throughout the city: fresh-caught Dungeness crab, Petrale sole, Point Reyes oysters and clams, calamari, rock cod, and wild salmon. The fresh seafood available in the city makes for tasty *cioppino* (a fish stew that originated here), clam chowder, and mixed grills. Although Fisherman's Wharf restaurants are pricey, some of the long-established places, such as Scoma's (see p101), offer good value, and serve legendary seafood right off their own boats.

With the city's high-tech economy on the rise, menu prices are rising, too. Fortunately, the city is also loaded with reasonably priced ethnic restaurants, neighborhood bistros, and deli cafés. Savvy travelers order the prix-fixe specials, eat tapas in bars during happy hour, and check out food trucks in the weekly **Off the Grid** market gatherings. Excellent restaurant reviews, ranging from elegant to affordable eateries and covering every type of ethnic variety, can be found on the **SF Gate** website. These reviews are also searchable by neighborhood. **Tablehopper** offers a free weekly column about the San Francisco dining scene. At the most famous restaurants in the city, reservations are a must, often days or even weeks in advance. **OpenTable** makes it easy to browse restaurants by type, location, and availability, then make reservations online.

Trips and Tours

Taking an organized trip or tour is a popular way to get around and see as much of the city and its surrounding areas as possible. The choice of such tours is plentiful. **Big Bus San Francisco** offers multilingual, hop-on-hop-off, open-top bus tours of the main attractions of the city. **San Francisco Whale Tours** sail under the Golden Gate Bridge to a vast Marine Sanctuary to see whales and sea turtles. **Alcatraz Cruises** offer narrated ferry rides and a multilingual audio walking tour of the island. For free walking tours of the city led by savvy locals and historians, try **San Francisco City Guides**. For on-foot explorations of the Presidio, hidden stairways, urban forests, and hilly neighborhoods, **Urban Hiker San Francisco** is a good bet. **Edible Excursions** offers culinary strolls through Ferry Building Marketplace, the Mission District, and Japantown, as well as seasonal trips to West Marin. The tour guides offer insight into the culinary background of each area, with stops along the way to taste samples. For craft beer lovers, **Bay Area Brewery Tours** shuttles people to breweries for talks and tastings.

Where to Stay

In recent years, San Francisco has seen many of its older properties transformed into themed boutique hotels, with examples including the rock-and-roll-themed Phoenix Hotel (see p147), the literary hideaway of the Hotel Rex (see p142), and the Beaux Arts landmark hotel The Marker (see p143).

A precious trove of the city's Victorian mansions now serve as splendid B&Bs. **Bed & Breakfast San Francisco** lists carefully selected private residences open to guests in every desirable neighborhood of San Francisco, including Pacific Heights and the

Marina, as well as farther afield in Marin County and the Wine Country.

Updated grand hotels, originally built before or shortly after the 1906 earthquake, are popular with visitors wanting an authentic San Francisco experience: the Fairmont, (see p145) The Westin St. Francis (see p144), the Palace Hotel (see p144), and the InterContinental Mark Hopkins (see p145) are all good choices.

In this international trading center and major convention city, high-rise hotels cater to a business clientele (which makes up more than a third of all hotel guests) with state-of-the-art electronics, multilingual staff, private voicemail, and commodious work spaces. The extra-secure "club" floors have separate elevators, private lounges and conference rooms, and complimentary food and drink, making them good places to entertain and meet with business colleagues. Over half of the lodgings in the city are within walking distance of the gigantic Moscone Center convention complex (see p35).

In one of the most popular cities in the world for tourism and business, hotels fill up during holidays, in the summer, and when big conventions are in town (which is often). Flexibility on dates is recommended, and to save money on accommodation, savvy visitors book hotels away from Fisherman's Wharf and Union Square, seeking bargains around the Civic Center, the Marina, Japantown, SoMa and Haight-Ashbury.

Parking is limited and expensive – most hotels charge $20–$50 to park overnight. Hotel breakfasts can be pricey, too, so if you see a deal that includes both, it is wise to grab it. B&Bs and smaller properties with fewer amenities can be around half the price of four-star hotels.

The cheapest stays, especially for families, are in dormitory-style rooms in hostels (see p148); private family rooms are also available. Hostels have common kitchens and laundry facilities, but bring your own linens or sleeping bags. Book well ahead, as California hostels are very popular. **Hostelling International** has a good selection on its website.

Headquartered in San Francisco and a popular choice of accommodation in nearly 200 countries, **Airbnb** connects home- and apartment-owners with travelers on a budget. The accommodations and their owners are user-reviewed on the website. Renting a room or an entire house from a local saves money and comes with invaluable insider advice and a friendly welcome. **Vacation Rentals by Owner** (VRBO) offers a similar service, while **Home Exchange** and **Invented City** allow homeowners to trade their homes at a time that is convenient to both parties.

DIRECTORY

DINING

Off the Grid
offthegridsf.com

OpenTable
opentable.com

SF Gate
sfgate.com

Tablehopper
tablehopper.com

TRIPS AND TOURS

Alcatraz Cruises
alcatrazcruises.com

Bay Area Brewery Tours
bayareabrewery
tours.com

Big Bus San Francisco
eng.bigbustours.com

Edible Excursions
edibleexcursions.net

San Francisco City Guides
sfcityguides.org

San Francisco Whale Tours
sanfranciscowhale
tours.com

Urban Hiker San Francisco
urbanhikersf.com

WHERE TO STAY

Airbnb
airbnb.com

Bed & Breakfast San Francisco
bbsf.com

Home Exchange
homeexchange.com

Hostelling International
norcalhostels.org

Invented City
invented-city.com

Vacation Rentals by Owner
vrbo.com

Places to Stay

Boutique Hotels

Hotel Rex

MAP P3 ▪ 562 Sutter St ▪ (415) 433-4434 ▪ www.viceroyhotelsand resorts.com ▪ $$
Steeped in the literary and artistic traditions of California, this great little hotel boasts an intellectual air and decor reminiscent of 1930s salon society. Still, the rooms have the latest touches, as well as writing desks for guests to pursue their own creativity. The hotel also hosts readings, art shows, and live music in the on-site Library Bar, where literary-themed cocktails are served.

Inn at the Presidio

MAP D2 ▪ 42 Moraga Ave ▪ (415) 800-7356 ▪ www. innatthepresidio.com ▪ $$
Housed in a historic building in the heart of Presidio, close to fabulous restaurants and museums, this elegant hotel has beautiful yet simple rooms.

Petite Auberge

MAP G3 ▪ 863 Bush St ▪ (415) 928-6000 ▪ www. petiteaubergesf.com ▪ $$
Located on Nob Hill, this French Provincial-styled hotel combines the luxurious and the rustic, with brass pans hung on the walls and pillow-top mattresses on the beds. As well as the complimentary breakfast buffet, there are freshly baked cookies every afternoon.

Clift Hotel

MAP P3 ▪ 495 Geary St ▪ (415) 775-4700 ▪ www. morganshotelgroup.com ▪ $$$
Possessing "equal parts wit, surrealism, and glamour," the proprietors of this Ian Schrager property, offer interior design by Philippe Starck. You'll laugh with delight at the visual jokes, including a surreal stool by René Magritte and a coffee table by none other than Salvador Dalí.

Enchanté Boutique Hotel

1 Main St, Los Altos ▪ (650) 946-2000 ▪ www. enchantehotel.com ▪ $$$
A favorite of Silicon Valley visitors, this stylish inn is modelled on a French château. It has luxurious amenities, including a library and canine concierge, and offers free breakfast, afternoon refreshments, and Wi-Fi. The charming on-site bistro serves dinner daily and brunch on Sundays.

Garden Court Hotel

520 Cowper St, Palo Alto ▪ (650) 322-9000 ▪ www. gardencourt.com ▪ $$$
The elegant, airy rooms in this Spanish-style hotel in downtown Palo Alto feature private terraces and marble bathrooms. Garden Court has consistently been named one of the best hotels in Palo Alto for many years. Some rooms also have fireplaces.

Hotel G

MAP P3 ▪ 386 Geary St ▪ (415) 986-2000 ▪ www.hotelgsanfran cisco.com ▪ $$$
Stay next to Union Square in sleekly designed rooms decorated in stylish greys and whites with wooden touches. The 2014 renovation of this 1908 building preserved many original features while adding modern comforts to rooms like free Wi-Fi, Smart TVs, honor bars, and Nespresso makers. The hotel shop sells chic clothing and objects for those who want to bring a piece of G home.

Hotel Kabuki

MAP F3 ▪ 1625 Post St ▪ (415) 922-3200 ▪ www.jdvhotels.com/ hotel-kabuki ▪ $$$
Enjoy Japanese hospitality in this boutique hotel in Japantown that features deep soaking baths, traditional gardens and a Zen-like ambience, which is enhanced by the efficient and friendly staff.

Hotel Triton

MAP P4 ▪ 342 Grant Ave ▪ (415) 394-0500 ▪ www. hoteltriton.com ▪ $$$
Perhaps the city's most original hotel, featuring avant-garde touches – evening tarot card readings, feather boa rental, and several suites designed by rock celebrities, including Jerry Garcia of the Grateful Dead fame. It's

all too cool for words; you might run into Cher or Courtney Love, both of whom have stayed here.

Hotel Zephyr

MAP K3 ▪ 250 Beach St ▪ (415) 617-6555 ▪ www.hotelzephyrsf. com ▪ $$$
A weird and wacky naval theme (think Popeye) give the lobby, guest rooms, and suites a humorous marine feel at Hotel Zephyr. The eclectic decor matches the waterfront Fisherman's Wharf location of this large, upscale but friendly hotel.

The Inn Above Tide

30 El Portal, Sausalito ▪ (415) 332-9535 ▪ www. innabovetide.com ▪ $$$
The only hotel built directly on the Bay. The views across the water from the private balconies in the guest rooms are stunning, and there is a serene ambience. This is a wonderful choice, convenient to the city via the Golden Gate Bridge or a ferry ride. Guests can borrow bicycles from the hotel free of charge.

The Marker

MAP P3 ▪ 501 Geary St ▪ (415) 292-0100 ▪ www. jdvhotels.com ▪ $$$
Situated in the heart of the Theater District, this quirky but extremely comfortable hotel is run to perfection. The fairy-tale decor is joyously original, being at once a celebration of color and elegance, and the beds may be the most comfortable in the world. The stylish restaurant is an attraction in itself, with polished oak and brass ornaments.

Mill Valley Inn

165 Throckmorton Ave, Mill Valley ▪ (415) 389-6608 ▪ www.marinhotels. com ▪ $$$
Combining the sophistication of a European hotel – tea is served all day – with the cozy charm of a Californian mill town, this intimate option is tucked away in a redwood grove.

Luxury Hotels

AC Hotel San Francisco Airport

1333 Veterans Bvd ▪ (650) 742-9211 ▪ www. achotelsfo.com ▪ $$
This chic Bayfront hotel is conveniently located just 10 minutes from both San Fracisco International Airport and Downtown. It is also close to the BART and Caltrain. It is equipped with a gym, restaurant, lounge, and indoor pool. Free parking, Wi-Fi and airport shuttles are provided. The hotel is adjacent to the 4-mile- (6-km-) long Bay Trail.

Four Seasons

MAP P4 ▪ 757 Market St ▪ (415) 633-3000 ▪ www. fourseasons.com ▪ $$$
Designed with the business expense-account traveler in mind, this place has amenities such as multi-line phones and free Wi-Fi in each room, and a well-run business center.

Hilton San Francisco Union Square

MAP P3 ▪ 333 O'Farrell St ▪ (415) 771-1400 ▪ www. hilton.com ▪ $$$
The three towers of this historic high-rise are found in the Theater District, near Union Square and the Moscone Center. Most rooms here offer spectacular views of either the city or the Bay. Cityscape bar and lounge, on the 46th floor, has the best panoramic views and there is also a 16th-floor pool deck.

Hotel Nikko

MAP Q3 ▪ 222 Mason St ▪ (415) 394-1111 ▪ www. hotelnikkosf.com ▪ $$$
High-tech and minimalist white marble interiors radiate modernity in this Japanese-style environment. Its cool comfort and tranquil luxury, with touches such as silk wallpaper, soothe the spirit and free the mind. The excellent Anzu restaurant creates the same peaceful atmosphere.

Hotel Vitale

MAP H2 ▪ 8 Mission St ▪ (415) 278-3700 ▪ www. jdvhotels.com ▪ $$$
The amenities reign supreme at this urban oasis looming above the city's spectacular waterfront. Check out your preferred style of pillow in the pillow library, attend a complimentary morning yoga class, relax in one of the outdoor rooftop soaking tubs, or enjoy luxury spa services.

Hyatt Regency

MAP N6 ▪ 5 Embarcadero Center ▪ (415) 788-1234 ▪ www.sanfrancisco regency.hyatt.com ▪ $$$
The 17-story atrium lobby, one of the largest in the world, has long plants cascading down from above, a waterfall, and glass elevators. A number of rooms and suites have either city or waterfront views.

JW Marriott

MAP P3 ■ 515 Mason St
■ (415) 771-8600
■ www.marriott.com
■ $$$

It's all about location at this large, elegant hotel situated in Union Square. Rooms have all modern amenities and a 24-hour butler service. Guests rave about the pillow-top mattresses. The service is top-notch and the beautifully furnished lounge areas in the lobby are welcoming and relaxing.

Loews Regency

MAP N5 ■ 222 Sansome St ■ (415) 276-9888
■ www.loewshotels.com
■ $$$

Located on the top 11 floors of the third tallest building in Downtown, this is one of the classiest hotels you'll find in San Francisco. It offers splendid views over the Bay and city. There are also added complimentary amenities such as free Wi-Fi, housekeeping with turndown service twice daily, and use of the house car.

Le Méridien

MAP N5 ■ 333 Battery St
■ (415) 296-2900 ■ www.
starwoodhotels.com
■ $$$

Sleek and sophisticated, Le Méridien is an elegant hotel, with many of the rooms offering views over the Bay. Its restaurant, Park Grill, serves American cuisine and has a lovely patio for al fresco dining. The terrace is also a great place to enjoy drinks. The service is first-class.

Palace Hotel

MAP P5 ■ 2 New Montgomery St
■ (415) 512-1111
■ www.sfpalace.com
■ $$$

Dating from 1875, this historic landmark hotel emanates architectural splendor. The gorgeous Garden Court (where traditional afternoon tea is served) and the original Maxfield Parrish mural in the Pied Piper bar are national treasures. The rooms are wonderful and varied in terms of design, but many do not offer views.

Sir Francis Drake

MAP P4 ■ 450 Powell St ■ (415) 392-7755
■ www.sirfrancis drake.com ■ $$$

This splendid Art Deco landmark is situated just a block away from Union Square. The doormen wear Beefeater costumes and the cable cars glide by constantly. All in all, it has a very festive and colorful feel to it, both in the private rooms and in the bistro and two bars.

Taj Campton Place

MAP P4 ■ 340 Stockton St ■ (415) 781-5555
■ www.tajhotels.com
■ $$$

A member of the Leading Hotels of the World and definitely one of San Francisco's finest, this place aims to provide personal attention to each of its guests. Expect to find the best of everything here. The restaurant, serving California Cuisine, also enjoys national ranking.

W

MAP Q5 ■ 181 3rd St
■ (415) 777-5300
■ www.wsanfrancisco.
com ■ $$$

Talk about trendy in this town, and all conversations will inevitably lead to the W hotel. The decor is minimalist, but with luxury touches throughout. Rooms feature flat-screen TVs and mp3 stereos. The clientele that come here for drinks are chic trendsetters, too.

The Westin St. Francis

MAP P4 ■ 335 Powell St
■ (415) 397-7000 ■ www.
westinstfrancis.com
■ $$$

This grand San Francisco institution still shines in its public rooms, but it has become a tour-group mediocrity otherwise. Nonetheless, the views from the tower rooms are still phenomenal.

Hilltop Hotels

Hotel Sausalito

16 El Portal at Bridgeway, Sausalito ■ (415) 332-0700
■ www.hotelsausalito.com
■ $$

With a quirky back story, this inviting boutique hotel has sixteen luxurious rooms, with custom furnishings, and suites decorated in pastel hues that offer park and harbor views.

Queen Anne Hotel

MAP F3 ■ 1590 Sutter at Octavia ■ (415) 441-2828
■ www.queenanne.com
■ $$

Built in 1890, this old mansion has been lovingly refurbished according to Victorian taste. The rooms are individually decorated and filled with antiques. The continental breakfast is complimentary, and the morning newspaper too.

Claremont Hotel Club & Spa

41 Tunnel Rd, Berkeley ■ (510) 843-3000 ■ www.fairmont.com/claremont-berkeley ■ $$$

This country club-style resort in the Berkeley Hills was built in 1915 and still retains the feel of that era. There are business services, a fitness center, two pools, tennis courts, and views of the Golden Gate Bridge.

Fairmont

MAP N3 ■ 950 Mason St ■ (415) 772-5000 ■ www.fairmont.com ■ $$$

"Opulent" and "palatial" barely begin to describe this *grande dame* of San Francisco's hotels, taking pride of place on Nob Hill. The rooms and service are commensurate with its superior status.

Hotel Drisco

MAP E2 ■ 2901 Pacific Ave ■ (415) 346-2880 ■ www.hoteldrisco.com ■ $$$

This Pacific Heights property has won many top hotel awards through the years, and, although the elegance is perhaps a little understated, it delivers on service. Details include complimentary continental breakfast and morning newspaper, as well as some of the very best vistas San Francisco has to offer.

InterContinental Mark Hopkins

MAP N3 ■ 999 California St ■ (415) 392-3434 ■ www.ihg.com ■ $$$

The Top of the Mark restaurant is a major pull, with its 360-degree panoramic views of the city, and the service is genuinely caring. The rooms are provided with every amenity and achieve an excellent standard of comfort.

Laurel Inn

MAP E3 ■ 444 Presidio Ave ■ (415) 567-8467 ■ www.jdvhotels.com ■ $$$

This stylish hotel is located in Presidio Heights, and is decorated in a hip mid-century fashion. Some rooms feature kitchenettes, and they all come with flat-screen TVs and Blu-Ray players. Breakfast, daily newspapers and refreshments in the lobby are included.

The Ritz-Carlton

MAP N4 ■ 600 Stockton St ■ (415) 296-7465 ■ www.ritzcarlton.com ■ $$$

Experience the ultimate in luxury and service at this hotel. Views from the rooms are magnificent, the staff are at the top of their game, and the food is nothing short of sublime.

The Scarlet Huntington

MAP N3 ■ 1075 California St ■ (415) 474-5400 ■ www.thescarlethotels.com ■ $$$

Situated at the top of Nob Hill, across from Grace Cathedral, this hotel feels like the clubby apartment of a rich uncle with impeccable taste. The rooms are luxurious and there's

an excellent restaurant, plus a spa where you can get a caviar facial.

Stanford Court

MAP N3 ■ 905 California St ■ (415) 989-3500 ■ www.stanfordcourt.com ■ $$$

Long a business favorite, this hotel is situated near the top of Nob Hill, handy to everything Downtown. The stained-glass dome in the lobby gives it a grand feel. It is eco- and pet-friendly, and offers complimentary Wi-Fi and free bicycles for visitors.

Gay and Lesbian Hotels

Inn on Castro

MAP E5 ■ 321 Castro St ■ (415) 861-0321 ■ www.innoncastro.com ■ No air conditioning ■ $

The very friendly owner of this B&B seems to have thought of everything to make your stay in the heart of the Castro as pleasurable as possible. He's always ready with maps and advice on where to go. Housed in a beautifully-restored Edwardian building, comfort is key here. Bright rooms are decorated with art and plants.

The Willows Inn

MAP E4 ■ 710 14th St ■ (415) 431-4770 ■ www.willowssf.com ■ No en-suite bathrooms ■ No air conditioning ■ $

This Edwardian house is conveniently located close to public transport links in the gay Castro District. The interior decor is a blend of handcrafted willow furniture, antique dressers. Kimono-style bathrobes are also provided.

Beck's Motor Lodge

MAP F4 ▪ 2222 Market St
▪ (415) 621-8212 ▪ www.
becksmotorlodge.com
▪ $
Basic but modern
rooms are on offer
in this renovated no-
smoking lodge with
a private sun deck, as
well as free parking
and Wi-Fi. Situated in a
lively area of the city, it
is popular with gay men.

Bel Abri

837 California Blvd, Napa
▪ (707) 253-2100 ▪ www.
belabri.net ▪ $$
Rooms in this Wine
Country inn have shutters,
French tapestries, and
wrought-iron features.
Most rooms also include
a fireplace, and two of
them have Jacuzzis.

Chateau Tivoli

MAP E3 ▪ 1057 Steiner St
▪ (415) 776-5462
▪ www.chateautivoli.com
▪ No air conditioning ▪ $$
Rooms and suites in
this stunning old building
are named after Mark
Twain, Enrico Caruso,
Jack London, and others,
to remind guests of San
Francisco's illustrious
history. Rooms have four-
poster beds and feature
decorative fireplaces
and bay windows.

The Inn San Francisco

MAP F5 ▪ 943 South Van
Ness Ave ▪ (415) 641-0188
▪ www.innsf.com ▪ No air
conditioning ▪ $$
This fine Victorian
mansion serves a
buffet breakfast in
charming parlors. The
garden has a redwood
hot tub, plus a sundeck
with a panoramic view
of the city.

The Parker Guest House

MAP F5 ▪ 520 Church St
▪ (415) 621-3222 ▪ www.
parkerguesthouse.com
▪ No air conditioning ▪ $$
An Edwardian mini-
mansion, located just
steps away from various
gay bars and restaurants,
this guesthouse has
expansive gardens
and sun decks.

Meadowlark Country House

601 Petrified Forest Rd,
Calistoga ▪ (707) 942-5651
▪ www.meadowlark
inn.com ▪ No air
conditioning ▪ $$$
In the heart of the Wine
Country, this elegant guest-
house is situated on an
estate with great facilities
such as a mineral water
hot tub and heated pool,
and a Finnish dry sauna.

Neighborhood Hotels

Pacific Heights Inn

MAP F2 ▪ 1555 Union St
▪ (415) 776-3310 ▪ www.
pacificheightsinnsf.com
▪ No air conditioning ▪ $
Set on a quiet block close
to public transport links,
this motel offers basic but
comfortable rooms. There
is free on-site parking,
Wi-Fi, and a continental
breakfast. Some rooms
also feature kitchens.

Seal Rock Inn

MAP A3 ▪ 545 Point Lobos
Ave ▪ (415) 752-8000
▪ www.sealrockinn.com ▪ $
This inn is in a handy
location for visiting Cliff
House and Land's End
(see p117), as well as the
Legion of Honor. Rooms
are large, though plain,
and there's a sun deck,
table tennis and outdoor

pool for the summer
months. Free parking
is available.

Hotel Carlton

MAP F3 ▪ 1075 Sutter St
▪ (415) 673-0242 ▪ www.
jdvhotels.com ▪ No air
conditioning ▪ $$
With a charming "National
Geographic" theme, this
European-style hotel is
a few blocks from Union
Square. Parking is avail-
able across the street
for $35. Don't miss the
free wine hour and
the on-site café.

Hotel Del Sol

MAP E2 ▪ 3100 Webster
St ▪ (415) 921-5520
▪ www.jdvhotels.com
▪ $$
Described as "festive and
spacious," this boutique
hotel is a ray of sunshine.
Bright colors and cheerful
patterns greet you around
every corner, and the staff
are just as nice as can be.
This is an especially great
place to stay if you are
traveling with kids.

Marina Motel

MAP E2 ▪ 2576 Lombard St
▪ (415) 921-9406 ▪ www.
marinamotel.com ▪ $$
Tucked away in a flower-
filled Mediterranean
courtyard decorated with
murals, this motel offers
guests a peaceful oasis
right in the heart of the
beautiful Marina District,
close to restaurants
and public transport
links. Rooms are simple
and clean, and parking
is included.

Metro Hotel

MAP E4 ▪ 319 Divisadero
St ▪ (415) 861-5364 ▪ www.
metrohotelsf.com ▪ $$
This conveniently located,
family-owned boutique

hotel is housed in a vintage Victorian walk-up (there are no elevators). The comfortable rooms are minimalist and all have private bathrooms. Guests can relax in the lush private garden.

Stanyan Park Hotel
MAP D4 ■ 750 Stanyan St ■ (415) 751-1000 ■ www. stanyanpark.com ■ No air conditioning ■ $$
Listed on the National Register of Historic Places, this Victorian hotel has been receiving guests since 1904. It is located right on Golden Gate Park and is decorated in period style. The hotel is known for its generous continental breakfast spread, along with free Wi-Fi, and a front desk that operates around the clock.

Jackson Court
MAP F2 ■ 2198 Jackson St ■ (415) 929-7670 ■ www. jacksoncourt.com ■ $$$
Located in the Pacific Heights area, this is a magnificent 1900 brownstone mansion. The wood-paneled parlor is an inviting place, and the stone fireplace provides a warm glow in which to enjoy afternoon tea.

Phoenix Hotel
MAP Q2 ■ 601 Eddy St ■ (415) 776-1380 ■ www. jdvhotels.com ■ $$$
Johnny Depp and the late John F. Kennedy, Jr have all stayed in this retro-style motorlodge, with a courtyard pool. Despite the glitzy clientele, it is located close to the gritty Tenderloin area, which is only for the most self-assured. Continental breakfast is included and the

restaurant/bar attracts trendy crowds from all across the city.

Pier 2620
MAP K3 ■ 2620 Jones St ■ (415) 268-5925 ■ www. pier2620hotel.com ■ $$$
Located in the buzzing Fisherman's Wharf area, a short walk from Pier 39, and with lots of shops and restaurants on the street, this hotel offers comfortable rooms. Street noise can be an issue, so ask for a room facing the courtyard if you are a light sleeper.

B&Bs and Guesthouses

Hayes Valley Inn
MAP F3 ■ 417 Gough St ■ (415) 431-9131 ■ www. hayesvalleyinn.com ■ $
A budget B&B option, but with a certain charm. The basic rooms have shared bathrooms.

The Red Victorian
MAP E4 ■ 1665 Haight St ■ (415) 864-1014 ■ www. embassynetwork.com ■ No air conditioning ■ $
Inspired by hippie ideals, this hostel encourages its guests to engage in intelligent conversation around the breakfast table at the "Peace Café." Each guest room is also designed to celebrate love.

Cliff Crest Inn B&B
407 Cliff St, Santa Cruz ■ (831) 427-2609 ■ www. cliffcrestinn.com ■ No air conditioning ■ $$
Surrounded by redwoods, the rooms in this Queen Anne Victorian are graced with fresh flowers, and some also have views over the Bay.

Gables Inn
62 Princess St, Sausalito ■ (415) 289-1100 ■ www. gablesinnsausalito.com ■ No air conditioning ■ $$
A luxurious, 14-room B&B with Bay views, this hotel is the perfect spot for a romantic break. Suites are available.

Golden Gate Hotel
MAP B4 ■ 775 Bush St ■ (415) 392-3702 ■ www. goldengatehotel.com ■ $$
Combining Edwardian charm with modern amenities, this hotel is one of the best small guesthouses within the city. It is family-run, with small, but luxurious, rooms. Tea and freshly baked cookies are available every afternoon.

Mountain Home Inn
810 Panoramic Hwy, Mill Valley ■ (415) 381-9000 ■ www.mtnhomeinn.com ■ $$
Step out of the door of this quaint mountainside inn and be blown away by the spectacular views it has of San Francisco Bay and Mount Tamalpais. Situated just 20 minutes from Downtown, this hikers' paradise invites you to meander to the beachside town of Stinson or to historic Muir Woods. Afterward, indulge in a hearty gourmet meal.

The Pelican Inn
10 Pacific Way, Muir Beach ■ (415) 383-6000 ■ www.pelicaninn.com ■ No air conditioning ■ $$
Majestically positioned deep in a valley, each of the seven rooms has antiques, and a roaring fire is lit every day in the inglenook fireplace.

Sleep Over Sauce
MAP F4 ■ 135 Gough St
■ (415) 621-0896
■ www.sleepsf.com
■ No air conditioning
■ $$
This boutique guest-house is a great find in the bustle of the city. The eight rooms are clean, modern, and comfortable. Also present is a common room to relax in and a business centre for work. Its restaurant, Sauce, is award-winning.

The Union Street Inn
MAP E2 ■ 2229 Union St
■ (415) 346-0424 ■ www.unionstreetinn.com ■ $$
Combining the elegance and gentility of a grand Edwardian home, this inn is located just up from the Marina and right on fashionable Union Street. The individually decorated rooms are all spacious, with original antiques and art, fine linens, fresh flowers, and compliment-ary chocolates and fruit.

Cavallo Point Lodge
601 Murray Circle,
Fort Baker, Sausalito
■ (415) 339-4700
■ www.cavallopoint.com
■ No air conditioning
■ $$$
A former military base, this luxury lodge has the charm of a B&B and is set in beautiful surround-ings at the foot of the Golden Gate Bridge. Rooms are comfortable and spacious.

White Swan Inn
MAP N3 ■ 845 Bush St
■ (415) 775-1755
■ www.whiteswaninnsf.com ■ $$$
This quaint B&B is like a country inn in the heart of Downtown,

with bright floral prints, Victorian-style canopied beds, and cozy fireplaces. An evening wine reception and English breakfast are both complimentary.

Budget Hotels

Coventry Inn
MAP F2 ■ 1901 Lombard St ■ (415) 567-1200
■ www.coventrymotorinn.com ■ $
A good, basic motel, offering large, plea-sant rooms with bay windows, located on the Marina's "Motel Row." It isn't beautiful, but it's functional and reliable. Wi-Fi and parking is compli-mentary. A minimum stay may apply on some weekends.

Hostelling International Downtown
MAP P3 ■ 312 Mason St
■ (415) 788-5604
■ www.sfhostels.org
■ No en-suite bathrooms
■ No air conditioning ■ $
This location is the perfect base for all the major sights. Rooms hold up to five beds. All major public transportation is just outside and there's lots of tourist information available, too.

Hostelling International Fisherman's Wharf
MAP F1 ■ Fort Mason, Building 240 ■ (415) 771-7277 ■ www.sfhostels.org
■ $
This hostel offers free breakfast, Wi-Fi, and parking. It's just a short walk to every-thing along the Bayshore. It is surrounded by a National Park on one

side and provides breathtaking views of the Bay.

Inn at the Opera
MAP F3 ■ 333 Fulton St
■ (866) 723-9878 ■ www.shellhospitality.com
■ No air conditioning ■ $
These 48 studios and suites are walking distance from the War Memorial Opera House Civic Center, City Hall, and the Louise M. Davies Symphony Hall. Each apartment offers a kitch-enette, free breakfast, and Wi-Fi. There is also an on-site café and bar.

Inn on Broadway
MAP E3 ■ 2201 Van Ness Ave ■ (415) 776-7900
■ www.broadwaymanor.com ■ $
All rooms at this no-smoking inn feature flat-screen TVs, and coffee-and tea-making facilities. Free parking and Wi-Fi. The location is an added advantage, as many of San Francisco's eye catching sites are within walking distance from the inn.

Marin Headlands Hostel
Fort Barry, Building 941, Field & Bunker Rds
■ (415) 331-2777
■ www.norcalhostels.org
■ No en-suite bathrooms
■ No air conditioning ■ $
Dorms and private rooms, some for families, near Muir Woods and beaches.

San Francisco Zen Center
MAP F4 ■ 300 Page St
■ (415) 863-3136 ■ www.sfzc.org ■ No en-suite bathrooms ■ No air conditioning ■ $
The Zen Center has several comfortable, quiet

rooms available for those who are interested in learning more about Zen practices and Buddhist techniques of meditation.

The Cartwright Hotel

MAP B4 ▪ 524 Sutter St ▪ (415) 421-2865 ▪ www.cartwrightunion square.com ▪ $$
This pet-friendly hotel has a fireplace in the lobby, simple rooms, and free Wi-Fi. It also has a great location, near the Theater District.

Cow Hollow Inn and Suites

MAP E2 ▪ 2190 Lombard St ▪ (415) 921-5800 ▪ www. cowhollowmotorinn.com ▪ $$
Larger-than-average rooms, with floral wallpaper and traditional furniture giving them a homey feel. Some suites have Oriental carpets accenting wood floors, marble fireplaces, and antiques.

Hotel Griffon

MAP H2 ▪ 155 Steuart St ▪ (415) 495-2100 ▪ www.hotelgriffon.com ▪ $$
Situated on the Embarcadero near the Ferry Building, this European-style hotel has 62 rooms. Perry's restaurant and bar serves American comfort food. Free Wi-Fi available.

The Mosser

MAP Q4 ▪ 54 4th St ▪ (415) 986-4400 ▪ www.themosser.com ▪ No air conditioning ▪ $$
It's hard to beat this location, less than a block from the center of Market Street and the nearest subway station. The Mosser has a few other things going for it as well – clean, Ikea-furnished rooms, great prices, and free morning coffee, tea, and muffins in the lobby.

San Remo Hotel

MAP K3 ▪ 2237 Mason St ▪ (415) 776-8688 ▪ www.sanremohotel.com ▪ No en-suite bathrooms ▪ No air conditioning ▪ $$
North Beach's biggest bargain is full of charms. Each room is decorated with antiques, and the corridors feature brass railings and hanging plants under skylights. Every room has its own sink, while the other bathroom facilities are down the hall.

Apartments and Private Homes

The Gateway

MAP N6 ▪ 460 Davis Court ▪ (866) 270-9902 ▪ www.thegateway.com ▪ $
Location is everything at these fully furnished apartments, which are just steps away from a host of retail stores, restaurants, and local transportation options. Offering every amenity and service one could possibly want when planning a long visit, these apartments promise a convenient and comfortable stay.

Monroe Residence Club

MAP N1 ▪ 1870 Sacramento St ▪ (415) 474-6200 ▪ www. monroeresidenceclub. com ▪ No air conditioning ▪ $
Amid the mansions of Pacific Heights, the Monroe combines the best elements of a hotel and an apartment. American-style breakfasts and four-course dinners are included. Maid service is also provided.

Casa Luna

MAP E5 ▪ 4058 17th St between Market & Castro ▪ (415) 738-8121 ▪ www.casalunasf.com ▪ No air conditioning ▪ $$
This restored Edwardian building has been converted into two luxury apartments in the heart of the Castro district. It boasts eco-friendly, stylish furnishings, Egyptian cotton sheets, and Jacuzzi soaking tubs. Each apartment has two bedrooms and two full baths in a very safe location.

One Pine Street

MAP N6 ▪ 1 Pine St at Market ▪ (877) 902-0832 ▪ www.oakwood.com ▪ No air conditioning ▪ $$
With a minimum stay of 30 days and starting prices lower than most hotels, these apartments offer one- and two-bedroom options, all with private balconies and equipped kitchens. Many have views of the Bay Bridge and the Financial District.

The Suites at Fisherman's Wharf

MAP F1 ▪ 2655 Hyde St ▪ (800) 227-3608 ▪ www.extraholidays.com ▪ $$
An easy walk to Fisherman's Wharf and public transport, this apartment hotel offers 24 one- and two-bedroom suites, with amenities that include kitchenettes, dining and living areas, and balconies.

For a key to hotel price categories see p142

General Index

Acknowledgments

Author
Native San Franciscan Jeffrey Kennedy now lives mainly in Italy and Spain. A graduate of Stanford University, he spends his time producing, writing, and acting. He is also co-author of *Top 10 Rome* and author of *Top 10 Mallorca* and *Top 10 Miami & The Keys*.

Additional Contributor Karen Misuraca

Publishing Director Georgina Dee

Publisher Vivien Antwi

Design Director Phil Ormerod

Editorial Michelle Crane, Rachel Fox, Fíodhna Ní Ghríofa, Freddie Marriage, Sally Schafer, Scarlett O'Hara, Anna Streiffert, Christine Stroyan

Design Richard Czapnik, Fatima Jamadar

Picture Research Phoebe Lowndes, Susie Peachey, Ellen Root, Oran Tarjan

Cartography Uma Bhattacharya, Simonetta Giori, Suresh Kumar, Casper Morris, James Macdonald, Reetu Pandey

DTP Jason Little, George Nimmo, Joanna Stenlake

Production Nancy-Jane Maun

Factchecker Lauren Viera

Proofreader Sam Cook

Indexer Hilary Bird

Illustrator chrisorr.com

First edition created by Sargasso Media Ltd, London

Revisions Subhadeep Biswas, Rebecca Flynn, Bharti Karakoti, Sumita Khatwani, Rahul Kumar, Hayley Maher, Alison McGill, Akshay Rana, Anuroop Sanwalia, Ankita Sharma, Rituraj Singh, Neil Simpson, Hollie Teague, Lisa Voormeij

Commissioned Photography
Christopher P Baker, Peter Anderson, Lee Foster, Robert Holmes, Britta Jaschinski, Neil Lukas, Andrew McKinney, Susanna Price, Rough Guides/Nelson Hancock, Rough Guides/Martin Richardson, Rough Guides/Paul Whitfield, Robert Vente.

Picture Credits
The publisher would like to thank the following for their kind permission to reproduce their photographs:
(**Key:** a-above; b-below/bottom; c-centre; f-far; l-left; r-right; t-top)

4Corners: SIME/Maurizio Rellini 14-5c; Susanne Kremer 120-1.

Absinthe Brasserie & Bar: Postcard PR 107tr.

Alamy Images: Mark Bassett 50tl; Jan Butchofsky 25cra; Felix Choo 88b; Danita Delimont 62t; Design Pics Inc/Laura Ciapponi 27b; Directphoto Collection 78br; Randy Duchaine 18cr, Dianne Feinstein statue by Lisa Reinertson 43bl; Enlightened Images/Gary Crabbe 119cl; Seth Grant 14bl; Michael Halberstadt 104bl; Dave G. Houser 63cla; Bob Kreisel 61cra, 67tr; Jackie Link 46bc; Jerome Brunet / ZUMA Press 71tr; Stefano Politi Markovina 1b, 4crb; Mountain Light/Galen Rowell 12br; Eric Nathan 23clb; Nikreates 68t, 69cl, 80t; North Wind Picture Archives 42bl; Wiliam Perry 35bl; PhotoBliss 116tl; The Print Collector 42t; Robert Rosenblum 27cr; Leonid Serebrennikov 92br; Stars and Stripes 64b; ZUMA Press, Inc 27tr.

Asian Art Museum: Orange Photography 52b.

AWL Images: Stefano Politi Markovina 4t.

Blue Bottle Cafe: Claypix.com/Clay McLachlan 76bl.

California Academy of Sciences: Tim Griffith 26br; Chris Picon 27tl.

Cliff House: 75tr.

Courtesy of the Contemporary Jewish Museum, San Francisco.: Bruce Damonte 33tr.

Corbis: Morton Beebe 23tl; Bettmann 21tr; Gerald French 90-1; Historical 47tr; Masterfile/Jose Luis Stephens 32tl; Proehl Studios/Steve Proehl 2tl, 8-9, Mural in the Beach Chalet at Ocean Beach by artist, Lucien Labaudt 51br; San Francisco Chronicle 13tl; Phil Schermeister 49tr; Marco Simoni 3tl, 84-5; Sunset Boulevard 20crb; Captain W. Swasey 88cla; Wonwoo Lee 15br.

de Young Museum: 29bl; Gregory Bertolini 28-9c; Painting of Boatmen on the Missouri George Caleb Bingham 29tl; Henrik Kam 28cla.

Delfina Restaurant: Eric Wolfinger 115b.

Dorling Kindersley Ltd: Courtesy of Grace Cathedral 87br, Jack London statue by Cedric Wentworth 44c; Willie Mays statue by William Behrends at AT&T Park 109tc; Courtesy of the Natural History Museum, London/Tim Parmenter 128cb.

Dreamstime.com: Brandon Bourdages 82cla; Canbalci 10-1t; Chee-onn Leong 59t; Cminor 58b; Kobby Dagan 82br; Drserg 53cr; Efaah0 17cr; F8grapher 19cr; Filiola 11tr; Friday 129cra; Gmargittai 25bc; Hviola 60tl; Issalina 12bl; Jabiru 18ca; Jackbluee 26cl; Jerryway 16-7c, 62cr; Jetjock 24-5c; Jewhyte 11cr; Jiawangkun 88cb; Scott Jones 89tl; Jpldesigns 48tl; Kazmaniac 36-7c; Russell Linton 11ca; Luckydoor 96tl; Lunamarina 7br, 103t; Lyngbyvej 19cl; Maciejbledowski 18-9b; Martinmolcan 12-3c, 110bl; Andres Garcia Martin 56cl; Masterlu 109br; Meinzahn 17cb; MNStudio 64tl; Eli Mordechai 60bl; William Perry 48br; Photoquest 24bl; Povalec 10bc; Qweszxcj 6tr; Radekdrewek 16clb; Radkol 83tl; Rahurlburt 34cl; Ralfweber 4cra; Rfoxphoto 34bc; Robynmac 77tr; Romrodinka 5clb; Sborisov 3tr, 10cl, 132-3; Sf_smk 4bl; Spwkr 126t; Srongkrod 80br; Tasstock 104tr; Pamela Tekiel 18clb; Rudy Umans 32t; Un- fetteredmind 125t; Ventdusud 105cl; Vonshots 4cla; Walleyelj 46t; 16br; Wizreist 38tr; Wolterk 97t; Zhukovsky Sphinx statue by Arthur Putnam 28c, 36bl.

Exploratorium, www.exploratorium.edu: Gayle Laird 67cla.

The Fairmont, San Francisco: 70t.

The Fairmont Sonoma Mission Inn & Spa: 38cl.

Fillmore Jazz Festival: anupma/Denise Lamott Public Relations 83tr.

Courtesy of Fraenkel Gallery, San Francisco: 54bl.

Gayle's Bakery: Gayle's Bakery 131tr.

Getty Images: Richard Cummins 66t; De Agostini Picture Library 108tl; Glow Images, Inc 86tl; Hulton Archive 43tr; Izzet Keribar 94t; The LIFE Picture Collection/Ralph Crane 21bl; Tim Mosenfelder 81tr; Movie Poster Image Art 13cb; Radius Images 118b; Redferns/Daniel Boczarski 45cl, /RB 45tr; George Rose 34-35; Ezra Shaw 61tr; Sports Studio Photos 45bl; The Washington Post/John Cohen 44tl; WIN-Initiative Labyrinth artwork by Eduardo Aguilera formed of rocks overlooking ocean 117b; www.35mmNegative.com 98t; Barry Winiker 15tl.

Penguin
Random
House

Printed and bound in China

First published in Great Britain in 2003
by Dorling Kindersley Limited
80 Strand, London WC2R 0RL

Copyright 2003, 2018 © Dorling
Kindersley Limited

A Penguin Random House Company

18 19 20 21 10 9 8 7 6 5 4 3 2 1

Reprinted with revisions 2004, 2006,
2007, 2008, 2009, 2010, 2011, 2012,
2013, 2014, 2016 (twice), 2017, 2018

A CIP catalogue record is available
from the British Library.

ISBN 978 0 2413 1163 9

MIX
Paper from
responsible sources
FSC™ C018179

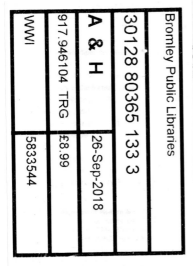

Top 10 San Francisco 2019 edit
5833544

Spruce: 75bl.

St. John Coltrane African Orthodox Church: 49cla.

Tacolicious: Aubrie Pick 101tr.

Tartine Bakery & Cafe: OpenKitchenPhotography/ Eric Wolfinger 76tr.

Trick Dog: Allison Webber Photography 114tr.

Yerba Buena Gardens: 57tr.

Cover
Front and spine – **Getty Images:** Mitchell Funk.
Back – **Robert Harding Picture Library:** P. Schickert.

Pull out map cover
Getty Images: Mitchell Funk.

All other images are: © Dorling Kindersley. For further information see www.dkimages.com.

*As a guide to abbreviations in visitor information blocks: **Adm** = admission charge; **D** = dinner; **L** = lunch.*

SPECIAL EDITIONS OF DK TRAVEL GUIDES

DK Travel Guides can be purchased in bulk quantities at discounted prices for use in promotions or as premiums. We are also able to offer special editions and personalized jackets, corporate imprints, and excerpts from all of our books, tailored specifically to meet your own needs.

To find out more, please contact:

in the US
specialsales@dk.com

in the UK
travelguides@uk.dk.com

in Canada
specialmarkets@dk.com

in Australia
penguincorporatesales@ penguinrandomhouse.com.au

Street Index